THE 3 ALARMS

A Simple System to Transform Your Health, Wealth, and Relationships Forever

ERIC PARTAKER

Published by Partaker International Limited

ISBN: 978-0-9903785-2-5

CONTENTS

Preface   ix

Part 1
FINDING THE PATH

1. Dying at 35,000 feet   3
2. Peak Performance Traps   14
3. Three Domains of a Fulfilled Life   25
    Part 1 Action Steps   35

Part 2
IPA: THREE KEYS TO PEAK PERFORMANCE

Overview   39
4. Identity-based Change   41
5. Productivity Planning   48
6. Productivity Execution   57
    Sample Quarterly Review   69
7. Antifragility: Stress Builds Strength   71
    Part 2 Action Steps   90

Part 3
THE THREE ALARMS

8. Introduction to The Three Alarms   95
9. The Healthiest You   101
10. The Wealthiest You   106
11. The Most Loving You   110
    Part 3 Action Steps   115

Conclusion: Living at the Summit   116
A Gift For You   119
3 Alarms Stories   121

Acknowledgements   127
About the Author   131

To my amazing wife Gisele and my incredible boys, Alex and Leo.

I love you forever.

PREFACE

DEAR READER,

Never have I felt the principles in this book to be more relevant than now. During the past year, I completed a challenging restructuring exercise with my company, only to see it face bankruptcy a few months later as a result of the COVID-19 pandemic. While it was ultimately rescued by new investors, the process was incredibly demanding.

So many other companies and people in the world haven't been as fortunate, perishing to the rapid spread of the virus. In these trying times, we must remain balanced, creating the success and wealth we desire through our work without sacrificing our health and relationships—and, as a matter of fact, while *improving* our health and relationships.

We do this by becoming the very best we're capable of being. We do this by optimizing ourselves for action. We do this by strengthening our ability to handle, and even benefit from, the unexpected. All of this is covered in the pages to come.

None of this came naturally to me. Sure, I've had my successes: advising Fortune 50 CEOs while at McKinsey & Company, helping build Skype's multi-billion dollar success story, and founding several businesses. But along the way, I almost died, my wife threatened to leave me, and I lost a company. The journey has been far from easy.

These pages contain over twenty-five years of trial and error, combining cutting-edge research with "in the trenches" experience. The lessons in this book have saved me in the past and are saving me again today. I'm convinced they can save you as well. Or, shall I say, I'm convinced they can propel you to a better future by helping you inch closer to your full potential.

The book is divided into three parts. Part 1 highlights that change is possible. Part 2 provides the principles to create that change. And Part 3 shows you how to implement and troubleshoot the principles on a daily basis so that you can create macro shifts in your life.

I believe we can all become extraordinary, without the unhealthy hustle, and that it's never too late to start. I hope this book helps you realize your full potential and transform your health, wealth, and relationships forever.

Warm regards,

Eric Partaker

London, United Kingdom

FINDING THE PATH

Part 1

1

DYING AT 35,000 FEET

In 2010, I flew from Spain to London with my friend and colleague Luis. At that point in my life, I had been going a mile a minute for over ten years, desperately wanting to grow my business and "be successful." But I wasn't even sure what that meant anymore.

Before boarding the plane, I felt unwell, and had been taken to the emergency room for some pain that had started in my chest and shot down my left arm. In the past, I had been to the doctor for chest and arm pains without any real diagnosis. They'd done various tests, but aside from high blood pressure, everything had come back fine. This time in Spain, however, the pain became unbearable. After the ambulance took me to the emergency room, I was given nitroglycerin to minimize the intensity and frequency of the pain.

At the airport, I called my insurance company to tell them about my emergency room visit, and mentioned I was still having symptoms. They connected me with a medical specialist who strongly advised me to not get on the plane. This seemed extreme. I had a business to run and wanted to get back home. Before the phone call ended, the specialist insisted once again, "So you're not going to get on that plane, right?"

"Right," I said and hung up. Luis looked at me and asked what they said. "They said I'm fine," I lied, and we boarded the plane. Soon after the cabin doors closed, my arm and chest pains increased.

As the plane ascended, Luis looked over and asked, "How are you feeling?"

"Not well," I said, meeting his eye and noticing a frozen expression on his face. Apparently, I didn't look well, either. Later, I learned Luis was having the same thought as me: this would be a terrible place for something bad to happen. As we reached cruising altitude, nausea set in, and I started sweating. At this point, my whole left arm was completely numb; it was ice cold, several degrees colder than the rest of my body. I asked my friend to feel for himself to make sure I wasn't overreacting. To his touch, it felt like a block of ice, like a dead person's arm. Luis looked scared.

"Can you ask someone for help?" I said.

Putting one hand on the seat in front of me and one on my seat, Luis jumped over me. He rushed to a flight attendant and asked her to come over. She asked about my symptoms, and I explained I had recently been to the hospital and had received nitroglycerin for my chest and arm pains. She immediately asked over the intercom if there was a doctor on board, and luckily for me, one came running up from the back of the plane. He put his finger to the left side of my neck and looked at his watch to take my pulse.

He felt my arm, looked up at the flight attendant and said, "We need to land this plane immediately. I think he's having a heart attack."

THE 2% CLUB

I have long been fascinated with the subject of peak performance. In high school, I learned that Abraham Maslow, the preeminent psychologist best known for creating the hierarchy of human needs, estimated that only two out of one hundred people reach their full potential. Only 2% of the population become everything they are capable of becoming. *Scary*, I thought, but alluring at the same time. I wanted to join this "club." In my mind, it would mean I'd made it, that I had succeeded.

To better understand what motivates human beings, Maslow proposed that we have five categories of needs: physiological, safety, love, esteem, and self-actualization. When a lower need is met, the next need on the hierarchy becomes the focus of our attention. Self-actualization, or the fulfillment of one's potential, is at the very top of the pyramid. And I was determined to get there. I believed that if I tried hard enough, I could become the best at whatever I chose to do. But my early years certainly hadn't proven this was true.

Throughout much of my childhood, I always felt mediocre no matter how much effort I put in. I had the work ethic, which I'd inherited from my parents who were always working hard to stay afloat in life. When I was growing up, my dad serviced and inspected air-conditioning units and eventually became a supervisor for the City of Chicago to do the same. My mom worked as a bartender before becoming a hairdresser and opening her own home salon. As a family, we always seemed to be working on a home improvement project of some sort.

In one particular house, we spent over five years redoing everything. We built a makeshift kitchen in the corner of our dingy little basement while we demolished and rebuilt various parts of our house. We added an extension, redid the roof, laid new flooring, constructed new walls, and installed all the electrical, just to name a handful of projects. Every single day one year, I would get home from school and work on the house. The hard-working, blue-collar work ethic I'd picked up from my parents meant I gave everything I did 110%, but in my quest to become my best, this didn't seem to work.

When I was fourteen, I transferred to St. Patrick's High School in Chicago and wanted to make the basketball team, but there was just one problem: I had never played a game in my life. And I didn't want to just make the team, of course; I wanted to be a starter, which was even more unlikely. There was no dissuading me, though. Academics came more easily to me than sports, so I bought a book called *Hoops,* thinking I could study my way into becoming a better basketball player. Every day, I woke up at 5:30 a.m., grabbed my ball, and dribbled all the way from my house to the local park, where I'd shoot around for about an hour before heading back home to get ready for school. I read the entire book and spent my sophomore year dutifully applying all of its principles.

The next year, I tried out and did, in fact, make the team. My performance, however, was abysmal. I played only a handful of games and never scored. Later on, the coach told me I'd made the team only because I had "such a big heart," which was a blow to my ego and made me wonder if all my hard work was ever going to pay off.

Academics, as mentioned, seemed to be more my thing. But even then, I would still struggle to understand things as quickly as the best students, ranking tenth in our small high school class, despite trying as hard as I could to reach the top spot. Initially inspired by Maslow's ideal of reaching my full potential, I became terrified I wouldn't live the life I was capable of, and this fear became my motivation.

Then, in college, I had my first peak-performance breakthrough. Sitting in class at the University of Illinois Urbana-Champaign, I heard the professor (who was visiting from Stanford) say, "If anybody gets a job at the company that I'm about to profile next, I'll fall out of my chair." I immediately perked up. The company he referenced was McKinsey & Company, the global management consulting firm. He went on to say they were the 800-pound gorilla of the consulting world. They hired only Ivy League graduates and NASA rocket scientists, he added, only half joking.

That was enough for me, and from then on, I was determined to land a job at McKinsey. I quickly learned that they didn't care just about grades but about extracurricular activities as well—so I joined the Finance Club at my university to start building up my resumé. At one of the club's first meetings, I spotted an opportunity. Every year, the Finance Club organized a field trip to a company, or rather a prospective employer, and the club's president asked who would like to take on that responsibility.

"I'll do it," I said quickly.

The very first thing I did the next day was call McKinsey's Chicago office. The woman who answered the phone and agreed to the trip turned out to be the Head of Recruitment.

I knew I wasn't going to be what they were looking for on paper, but I also knew myself and believed I could figure out a way to get in. A few months later, we went on the field trip, and shortly after that, I called up the recruiter to say how much we had enjoyed our time at McKinsey. "I was blown away by what I learned," I said, "and I'd love a shot at applying." Thankfully, or rather strategically, I'd already made a good impression, so she went ahead and passed my application along to the interview stage. But that was just the next step in the process. The real challenge would be making it through the nine grueling interviews that stood before me. I had come to learn that the McKinsey interview process was notoriously difficult, so I knew I'd need all the help I could get.

My mother suggested I speak with a friend of the family who worked at the University of Chicago's business school, so I reached out to her to see if she could help. I was eager to meet any graduate students who were trying to get jobs at consultancies similar to McKinsey. Our family friend made a few calls and then connected me with the President of the Management Consulting Club at the business school. Similar in nature to the Finance Club, this group helped its members land jobs at top-tier management consulting firms.

The club president introduced me to a few other club members, and over the next few months, I sharpened my McKinsey interview skills, regularly completing the 4.5-hour journey to and from the University of Chicago to practice interviewing. Specifically, I was trying to master the case interview—a particular type of interview, about 90 minutes in length, during which you're presented with an abstract mathematical or business problem to see how you would collect the information you needed to recommend a solution. Often, there is no right answer, and it's more a test of your problem-solving ability and intellect. With my newfound peers, I ran through over thirty practice case interviews. My rigorous practice, together with the connection I'd forged with McKinsey's Head of Recruitment, helped me navigate the nine interviews and land the job.

There were over 2000 applicants for twenty-two roles at McKinsey that year. Landing that job was the great equalizer for me. After years of trying to be a star athlete and valedictorian, I had finally proven I could achieve something reserved for the very best. I didn't go to an Ivy League school, and on paper should have never gotten the job, but I did. I had my first taste of the 2% Club, and that changed everything.

Little did I know that I had also taken my first step in a dangerous direction. In the years that followed, throughout my career as an entrepreneur and executive, I pursued greatness at work at the cost of everything else. Until I nearly died 35,000 feet in the air.

A WAKE-UP CALL

I don't want to die on this plane, I thought, as the pilot announced we'd be making an emergency landing in France. Landing that job at McKinsey had certainly felt like the start of a dream life, yet ten years later, here I was, about to lose everything.

Descending seemed to last an eternity, and I was terrified my heart would stop just before I reached safety. I certainly wasn't thinking of everything I'd accomplished or all the successes I'd experienced. Instead, I immediately thought of my five-year-old son, waiting for me at home. Maybe I'd joined the 2% Club when it came to my work, but that didn't matter when I thought I was about to die. What mattered was that I'd failed to prioritize my health and my son as much as my work. I didn't want to die having never been the best father I could have been for my boy.

As the pilot prepared to land the plane, the piercing chest pains continued. I felt equal amounts of fear and hope, worried it was going to be "lights out" for me before we even landed.

The runway was completely blocked off, and an ambulance was waiting when we arrived. A team of paramedics rushed onboard, instructing me to move as little as possible as they lifted me out of my seat. Carrying a six-foot-two, two-hundred-pound man over the aisles of people on the cramped plane was no easy task.

As the medics lifted me over the seats, I looked to my left and saw a family of three–a mother, daughter, and father– burst into tears. In the ambulance, the paramedics quickly administered nitrates to open up my arteries and increase the blood flow to my heart. Looking into the eyes of the French medic standing over me, I said, "Please don't let me die. I have a five-year-old son."

"Just relax," the medic said. "We're going to look after you."

I didn't know it then, but my life had probably just been saved.

Looking back on it now, I think that in moments like that, whatever comes out of your mouth is the truth. When you think it's game over and you're about to die, there's no time for premeditation. Though work might have appeared to be the most important thing in my life, it clearly wasn't. I didn't think about the emails awaiting my reply or the projects I needed to complete. At that moment, my heart spoke, and what it said unnerved me.

The next morning I woke up in a French hospital, alone. My friend Luis had gotten off the plane, too, but he'd slept in a different area of the hospital. It seemed like ages before a doctor came to see me. *How did I get here?* I thought. *What was I doing with my life? Had I said goodbye to my son when I left?* I thought of all the times he had asked me to play and I'd said no because I was busy with work. In fact, as I thought about it, that was most of the time.

My life then was a constant hamster wheel of achievement that came at the price of everything else. My friendships, my son, my body—it was all being sacrificed on the altar of so-called "success." But was it worth *this?* That experience was an alarm bell of the worst kind. My career wasn't the only area that demanded excellence and examination. My health and relationships deserved more from me, too.

Lying in that hospital bed, I knew I needed to make some big changes. I knew I couldn't let this happen again, because the next time I might not be so lucky. This was the end of viewing myself as indestructible. I'd experienced my first real taste of mortality, and it felt like I'd been given a second chance at life. I intended not to waste it.

You may not have had a health scare like I did, but nearly everyone experiences a wake-up call at some point, when we realize something needs to change. And if you haven't just yet and are running through life at a breakneck pace, believe me, if you don't change, your wake-up call is coming.

THE RULE OF MARGINAL GAINS

Change came slowly. It wasn't the flip of a switch, and I didn't immediately become better. But that terrifying moment started a journey of what they call "marginal gains" in British cycling lore.

In 2003, Dave Brailsford became the Performance Director for the British cycling team. After over 100 years of mediocrity, the team invited Brailsford to help them create small, marginal improvements over the course of one year. He started with obvious things like better bikes and seats, and he eventually found the best mattresses for sleep and taught his riders about proper hand washing to reduce the odds of getting sick. Brailsford believed that if you considered every single aspect about the bike and rider, finding a way to make tiny improvements across the board, you would get a significant increase in speed when you added everything up. The next year at the Olympics, Great Britain won two gold medals—all due to the collective power of small, tiny improvements.

Over the next decade, I changed my life in many of the same ways. The emergency landing of that plane launched a whole new way of living for me, one in which I decided to really commit to the 2% Club—not just at work, but also with my health and relationships. I wanted to be the best at what I did, but I redefined what "the best" meant. And my life has never been the same since.

This book is about what I learned, and the key peak-performance principles I integrated, to reach my full potential across the three domains of life—health, wealth, and relationships— which we all must optimize to become our best. I'll share pieces of my own story in hopes that it inspires you to change your life for the better, while introducing you to some of the world's leading experts on peak performance, motivation, and health. Hopefully, in reading this book, you won't have to make the same mistakes I made to learn these same lessons. I'll also share with you the simple system I used to change my life forever, and how something as simple as setting three alarms can alter the course of your entire life.

I believe we are all capable of becoming the best version of ourselves, without the unhealthy hustle, and that it's never too late to start. If the idea of joining the 2% Club resonates with you, and if you have ever wondered if you have more to offer but are scared of the costs, this book is for you.

I've failed at many things in my life, but through this journey, I've learned what a life well lived looks like, and how it's accessible to anyone. That's not to say it's an easy path. The peak-performance journey can be dangerous if you don't look out for the traps along the way. But there is nothing like a life in which you live out your fullest potential.

I invite you to join me.

2

PEAK PERFORMANCE TRAPS

As an entrepreneur and executive coach, I often give talks and host workshops on the subject of peak performance and the topics in this book. In a recent session with Facebook's Global Learning team, I said, "Imagine I had a magic button, and if you press this button, it will instantly make you the best version of yourself. Would you push it?"

Of course, everyone always agrees that they would. Who wouldn't want to become the best version of themselves?

"So if it's a universal desire that we all have," I ask, "then what's the issue? Why do most people fail to become all they're capable of being?"

The answer is quite complicated and different for everyone. Everyone would love to reach their full potential, to perform at their best and reach the very top of Maslow's hierarchy. This is what I define as peak performance. Peak performers seek to become all they're capable of becoming, in the areas of life that matter most. They seek self-actualization. If peak performance is what we all want from our lives, we have to be mindful of the common traps we face on this journey. Almost certainly, you will encounter five obstacles as you pursue personal mastery. Let's look at each one.

TRAP #1: LACK OF INTENTIONALITY

When I first heard of Maslow's estimate, that only 2% of people reach their full potential, I felt terrified and liberated at the same time. It was a scary number, but I was still excited to become the very best version of me. I knew there must be some levers I could pull to get myself closer to this level of existence.

I thought of it like chemistry. What activation energy would be required to break free from that sticky pack of the 98%? What could I do to propel myself forward? Could I create some disproportionate force to break away? It turned out that I could, and you can, too. We have some control over our life and how it turns out; there are, in fact, forces to leverage.

The most simple but powerful of these forces is intentionality. It's amazing how few people actually stop and think about where they're going and how they're going to get there. If you don't make a plan for yourself, you're going to the shooting range in a blindfold. You aren't going to hit much, or at least you won't hit what you want. And you might get hurt walking around blind.

Author and entrepreneur Michael Hyatt calls this way of living "the drift." At some point you look up and find yourself somewhere completely different than where you thought you'd be in life. Like a person mindlessly caught in a riptide, you don't stop to evaluate where you're going and why—until it's perhaps too late. You'll just float through life, going nowhere at all—or at least not where you want.

Take the time to envision the best version of yourself and your life. Some people genuinely don't have an idea of what that is or believe they can get there. But more often than not, it's just that they haven't taken the time to think about it. In Part 2, we'll discuss some tools you can use to get yourself there faster, and it starts with deciding who you want to be.

Imagine you've been living in a kingdom under a tyrant for years. This dictator worked you day and night, and didn't allow you the freedoms you desired. Then one day a stranger walks up and says, "Did you know you could just move? There is a shallow river you can cross to enter the kingdom next door where everyone is free to do what they want." Intentionality is like that. There is a better way; you just have to decide to move.

TRAP #2: PERFECTIONISM

During our journey, we must focus on progress, not perfection. There is a Japanese proverb that states, "Fall down seven times, stand up eight." You will naturally make a lot of mistakes along the way. You'll start working out and miss a day. You'll get that promotion, but mess up your first project. You'll be helpful at home, but then get into an unnecessary argument. Just keep standing back up. As long as you keep standing up and learn from your mistakes, you'll keep making progress, and in a year you'll be much further down the path than you would have been if you'd quit the first time you fell.

Think about our shooting range example again. Sometimes you're going to hit the bullseye and feel great about it. But afterwards, don't expect to hit only bullseyes from there on out. It's just something to aim for. Sometimes you'll miss the target completely. Keep trying.

The more you brush it off and get back up, the easier it will become to laugh off your missteps. Even if you get derailed, you've laid down your tracks in the direction you want to go, and you'll get better at getting right back on. You know that track is taking you toward your best self. Remember: marginal gains.

People underestimate the power of taking small, imperfect actions regularly. Become an optimalist rather than a perfectionist, as author Tal Ben-Shahar discusses in *The Pursuit of Perfect*. Perfectionists live in a world where everything must be just right. Optimalists share the same high standards, but also embrace reality. They focus on progress, not perfection, knowing that all the marginal gains compound over time.

Make peace with the process, plateaus and all. There is a word I love that we'll cover at depth later in the book—antifragility—a concept popularized by Professor Nassim Nicholas Taleb. Someone who is antifragile grows stronger from stress, shocks, and failures. So don't try to be perfect. Get a little bit better every day, and when things go wrong, remember that stress builds strength.

TRAP #3: TOO MUCH STRUCTURE

Anticipating that our days will go exactly as planned is completely unrealistic. When my coaching clients become frustrated with their output or performance, it's often because they are not building enough buffer (or just general realism) into their day. I'll often ask them, "I know your day didn't go as expected, but in hindsight, did you do what needed to be done at the time?" The answer is almost always yes. We "win the day" not because we achieved what we planned, but because we did what was most important despite our plans.

Things come up. You had your ideal work day mapped out, but then an email about an urgent task arrives and it all goes out the window. Or perhaps you had a great workout planned, but your car breaks down, so you have to handle that first. Don't feel bad about yourself if you have to take care of the unexpected. As John Lennon once famously said, "Life is what happens when you are busy making other plans." Build some buffer into your day for the unplanned so you don't get derailed if things don't go as you'd like.

We will talk about mapping out the perfect day in chapter 5. But for now, just remember: if you did what needed to be done in the moment, despite your original plan, it's still a winning day. Don't let inflexibility get in the way of true productivity.

TRAP #4: PROCRASTINATION

Procrastination is an obvious obstacle to performing at our best, right? After all, if you don't do the work, you won't improve or accomplish your goals. Yet procrastination still seems to plague most of us.

I used to be a terrible procrastinator. I even had a collection of books about procrastination that I bought in 2000 and procrastinated on reading until 2010. I have always achieved a lot, but it came packaged with a lot of unnecessary stress and pain. Imagine how much progress I could have made if I had just picked up the books ten years earlier. One of those books was *The Now Habit* by psychologist Neil Fiore, and it changed my life. I was so moved by what I read, and so fed up with my procrastination habit, that I emailed Neil and hired him for sixteen one-on-one sessions to cure my procrastination. Neil taught me many things, and here are four in particular that helped transform me from a procrastinator to a producer.

Positive self-talk

One of the most impactful things Neil taught me was to examine how I spoke to myself when I procrastinated. When you feel yourself beginning to procrastinate, verbalize what's going on in your head at that moment. You'll probably be saying something along the lines of "I have to" or "I must." This is the language of oppression, Neil pointed out, and suggests you're being forced to do something you don't want to do. Being forced to do anything creates resistance, which manifests as procrastination.

Neil taught me to change from the *language of oppression*, negative self-talk, to the *language of choice*, positive self-talk. Whenever I felt the urge to procrastinate I would swap the "I have to" voice in my head with "I choose to." You may not want to do a particular task, but you can always still choose to do it. This choice creates agency, helping you feel in control. Since you're not being "forced" to do something, you're less likely to employ procrastination as a self-defense tactic.

———

Focus on starting

We also unknowingly trigger procrastination by focusing on finishing rather than starting. If you were to continue the "I have to" sentence in your head, it's often followed by the word "finish"— as in, "I have to finish writing this report." Focusing on finishing can be overwhelming, triggering procrastination once again. Instead build on your language of choice by focusing on starting for a small amount of time. Neil taught me to say the following to myself: "I choose to start for just five minutes." Do I actually stop working on a task after just five minutes? Only rarely.

If you can just get yourself to start, often you'll get absorbed in what you are doing and keep going. I call it "getting lost in the deep." A lot of writers and creators call it "flow." Whatever you want to call it, starting is the hardest part, and finishing often takes care of itself. It's all about creating momentum and continually finding moments to start.

As the saying goes, "The hardest part about running is putting on your shoes."

Centering

Before starting a period of quality, distraction-free work, I complete a sequence of deep breaths. It goes like this: first, take three breaths to relax. Then take three breaths to let go of the past, and another three to let go of the future. Lastly, take three breaths to remind yourself how easy it is to take a vacation in the present. You don't need to be anywhere or do anything other than what you're doing in that moment. Gently open your eyes to the task at hand, and choose to start for just five minutes. When I first learned this, I would have to constantly recenter every ten to fifteen minutes. It's much easier now, but it does take some rewiring of your brain. And if you stick with it, it works.

———

Guilt-free play

Scheduling your free time helps fight procrastination because it gives you something to look forward to. It also makes you aware of how little time you actually have. I'm much more likely to buckle down and get things done when I know I only have a few precious hours to work with. I also like knowing that, afterward, I get to do something fun like hang out with my family or friends.

Don't schedule just your fun time. Schedule your health time, break time, sleep, etc. You'll feel great knowing you've looked after yourself, while feeling more motivated to use your time productively.

TRAP #5: HYPERFOCUSING ON A SINGLE DOMAIN

The last, most common, and perhaps most insidious trap is hyperfocusing on only one domain of life.

For the CEOs, entrepreneurs, and leaders I coach, this is often their careers. But there are three areas of life that we must master, and our health and relationships deserve just as much attention as our work.

What would you be without your health, for example? Or your loved ones? I certainly had to face this reality.

Health, work, and relationships represent the three-legged stool that provides stability and meaning to our lives. Remove a leg, and the stool becomes imbalanced. Remove two, and life will be very wobbly indeed.

Adding or strengthening a leg creates improvements in the others as well. If you begin working out, you'll have more energy at work and a better attitude when you get home. You'll have more clarity and be better equipped to handle stress.

When you take a moment to stop and play with your kids or go on a date night with your spouse, I'm willing to bet you'll find more meaning and ambition in your career as well. Positive changes in one area creates positive changes in another.

Although work can easily dominate our attention, it is possible to be imbalanced towards your health and relationships as well.

Here are the three types of people who hyperfocus on one domain.

The Workaholic

This was me, and on my worst days, it still is. Workaholics prioritize their careers over everything else, which may lead to financial success and industry fame. Such a person is ambitious, and is usually rewarded for their intense effort and disciplined work ethic.

But their health and relationships suffer because of the hyper focus on work. Perhaps this describes you. Maybe you feel the strain from the demands at work. You're rarely at home, and when you are, you're unable to be completely present and focused. Maybe you lack a vibrant social life with no real friends or hobbies.

A lifetime as a workaholic can cost you your life and those you love the most. It almost did for me. As extreme as it sounds, I'm grateful for the wake-up call that stopped me from heading any further down this road.

———

The Martyr

The martyr hovers over family and friends at the expense of nearly everything else. This one might be harder to spot, because it seems noble to self-sacrifice. Maybe they're a homemaker, happily focusing all their energy on their kids or family, yet still longing to express themselves or shine in some other way.

This type likely hasn't worked out in months; perhaps, they quit their job to take care of children or a loved one, and now parts of their life feel unfulfilled. Don't get me wrong. These are worthy pursuits, and are often thankless. Caretakers of any kind should be praised for their important work, but they may have more they want to do and contribute to the world. If you find yourself relating to any of this, if your health and work feel unhealthily compromised by your relationships, you might be the martyr.

———

The Health Nut

The health nut prioritizes health and fitness over everything else. They work out all the time and obsess over what they eat, when what they really need is to relax and go out with a friend once in a while. Maybe their relationships are deteriorating because they come second to working out. Perhaps their career has suffered because they are so focused on their weight and physique. This is particularly dangerous because, taken to the extreme, the health nut can develop some very real physical and mental struggles that may require professional intervention.

You can pick your poison here because there are plenty of ways to get off balance. And, of course, there are times of exception, like in the days after you bring home a newborn, and it's a big win if everyone just makes it through the day, let alone eats properly and gets work done.

There will be times when you have a big project at work and may need to miss a workout or rearrange a date night. That's when the progress-over-perfection mindset comes in again. Do what you need to do, but always check in with yourself, and don't stay off balance for long. Plan a weekend off after that project is finished.

Pay for a bootcamp in advance so you know you can't miss it. Always keep in mind the need for balance, and don't hyperfocus on one area, like I did for years.

The realization that all three domains of my life were equally important and demanded equal attention was life-changing. I am much healthier, happier, and more successful today than I was ten years ago because I started giving equal priority to my health, work, and relationships. Think hard about whether you are hyperfocusing on one domain. Is your life out of balance somehow? It might not seem intuitive that focusing on your health or family will help you at work, but it will. A happy, healthy, well rested you is a more productive you.

3

THREE DOMAINS OF A FULFILLED LIFE

In 2018, Elon Musk told *The New York Times* he works 120 hours a week and sleeps an average of six hours a night. This means he works seventeen-hour days, seven days a week. He admitted to missing his own birthday party and that he could only spare a few hours away from the factory for his brother's wedding, flying in two hours before the ceremony and leaving shortly afterwards.

At the time of the article, Musk hadn't taken a week off of work since 2001, which was only because he had malaria. He says he sometimes spends the night in Tesla's factory, keeping a sleeping bag in a conference room next so that he can inspect vehicles as they come off the assembly line. During the interview, the reporter said the SpaceX founder alternated between laughter and tears.

"There were times when I didn't leave the factory for three or four days," he said, "days when I didn't go outside. This has really come at the expense of seeing my kids. And seeing friends." At this point, the interviewer notes that Musk stopped talking because he became overwhelmed with emotion.

Is this success?

A study in 2004 revealed that people who slept only six hours per night for two weeks straight functioned as poorly as those who had been awake for 48 hours. A person cannot operate at that level for very long—it's unsustainable and unhealthy. Still, many of us hold up these people on pedestals of achievement, often as examples of what we should strive towards.

Elon Musk is regarded by many as one of the best business leaders and entrepreneurs of our time. He is a coveted guest on television and podcasts; his recommendations and endorsements carry a lot of weight. His power and influence are without question. People want to be like him. But are people willing to pay the price he's paid for his success?

As we pursue our own greatness, we ought to be careful how much we idolize people who work 120 hours a week and sleep under their desks. Peak performance, though a worthy pursuit when properly understood, has a dark side that can ruin you. At some point, something has to give, or there will be grave consequences.

I found this out the hard way in 2010, having gotten everything I wanted, yet still feeling unfulfilled. I didn't have the fame and fortune of Musk, but I was suffering the same consequences of having too narrow a view of peak performance. Because I had no balance, I had no integration with the other important areas of my life. You can't expect to have a great life if work is the only thing you focus on.

TIME IS NOT ON YOUR SIDE

We have to understand that life cannot be compartmentalized. We must seek to integrate all aspects of our lives if we want to have a meaningful and fulfilling existence.

My coaching clients often believe they don't have time to make small improvements to their lives. But time is not on your side, and the small improvements can't wait. They have to start now. At the start of a coaching journey, my clients typically think, *I just need to get past this thing* or *I'll have more time once this season is over.* They often confuse surviving and thriving. They believe that because they have been surviving this way for so long, things are working just fine.

In reality, they've become accustomed to a lower baseline of productivity and happiness, and their lives are in danger of imploding.

I will often ask them, "Wouldn't you thrive if you got more sleep? Wouldn't you thrive if you were happier in your marriage?" Don't settle for the status quo just because it *seems* to be working. If you don't have time for the things you enjoy, you aren't thriving. If you aren't spending time with loved ones, you aren't thriving. If you fill your body with junk food because you don't have enough time or energy to care about your health, you aren't thriving. And all of this will catch up with you eventually.

Be careful thinking you will have time later, because as I learned, our time can run out at any moment. A stanza from "The Clock of Life" by Robert H. Smith puts it nicely:

The clock of life is wound but once,
And no one has the power
To tell just when the hands will stop
At late or early hour.

None of us knows how much time we have, so we must make the most of it right now. My early successes came at the price of my health and relationships. After the plane incident, I began making significant changes in my health. I created a healthier work/life balance, and my cardiologist said everything was looking great. But I wasn't out of the woods yet.

WHOLE-LIFE INTEGRATION

Before 2010, I worked hard but not smart. After that fateful emergency landing, I began re-evaluating how I showed up at work. I upgraded my confidence, leadership, and productivity, and also began focusing on my health, applying peak-performance habits to my well-being and not just my career.

I read lots of books and did plenty of research on how to work out, eat, and treat my body. It was another area where I could set ambitious goals and really excel. My health, and overall life, significantly improved and I thought I was doing everything right. But still, I was neglecting one important leg of the three-legged stool that supports a meaningful life: relationships.

I married my amazing wife Gisele in 2013, and she certainly helped me reevaluate my priorities and see what was truly important. Still, one morning a few years into our marriage she told me she was leaving. I had made real progress in my work and my health, but was balancing on a two-legged stool, which is not a very stable way to live. I still had not fully integrated peak performance principles into all arenas of my life.

It was another alarm bell, another wake-up call. Again I knew something had to change, in perhaps the hardest domain of life. I was performing at a high level at work, I had greatly improved my health, yet I still needed to become a better spouse and parent.

I believe peak performance and reaching your potential are about whole-life integration. As previously mentioned, there are three domains in life that are equally important and affect each other every day: our health, our wealth (or work), and our relationships. Neglect one, and you'll hurt the others. In my work as a coach, I don't usually have to convince CEOs and entrepreneurs to strive for mastery in their careers. I can help them be more productive and give them plenty of tactics for achieving their goals. They already want that and have been working toward it for a long time, but the blind pursuit of peak performance in one arena of life almost always means neglecting others.

The irony is that strengthening your health and relationships will almost certainly make you more successful in your career. If you are physically healthy, you are more likely to perform better at work. If your relationship with your spouse is strong, you will probably focus better. Though it may seem obvious, these three domains are much more interdependent than people realize.

Viktor Frankl called these domains relationships, work, and self. Frankl was an Austrian neurologist, psychiatrist, and Holocaust survivor, and one of the few people Abraham Maslow believed had reached self actualization. He was held captive in a few different Nazi labor camps, including the death camp Auschwitz.

After his liberation, Frankl wrote *Man's Search for Meaning*, about the people in concentration camps who had the greatest chance of survival. He noticed it wasn't just that people wanted to move away from their pain and toward pleasure, as Freud had taught, but also that they sought purpose in their relationships, work, and pain. If we, too, want to reach our potential, we must find time to focus on other people, dedicate our energy to work that matters, and find a way to make meaning out of our pain. This was true in the Nazi death camps, and it is still true today.

Brian Johnson, the founder of Optimize, a public benefit enterprise focused on self-actualization, often says that our work and love are deeply connected to our happiness and satisfaction. But Brian adds that without our health, as I painfully experienced firsthand, our work and love won't provide much fulfillment. So once again we must focus on all three domains—our health, work, and relationships—to live a happy and fulfilling life.

High-performance coach Brendon Burchard also recommends a wholly integrated life to reach our full potential. He's quick to point out that we shouldn't sacrifice our life outside of work for success within our work. When I've spoken with Brendon, he's defined a high-performing life as one in which you consistently experience success, over the long term, *without* sacrificing your health and relationships.

When I go deep with CEOs, entrepreneurs, and leaders, they don't want to be just high-performing leaders. They also want to be fit and be great spouses and parents. We intuitively understand the importance of taking a holistic view and how these areas are intimately connected. In sports for example, you don't achieve peak performance by just looking at what you do *on* the field. You also have to look at what you're doing *off* the field. Want to become a better leader? Start by becoming a better parent or by waking up early to work out. Remember the magic button I mentioned in Chapter 2 that could transform you into the best version of yourself? If you could push this button and instantly get a significant increase in energy and a fulfilling relationship, wouldn't you? Of course. We all would. You aren't a one-dimensional being; you are multidimensional, and you want a life that fulfills you in many different ways.

THE THREE ALARMS

In 2014, I read Charles Duhigg's *The Power of Habit* and was inspired to use the science of habit formation to better myself in each domain of life. The trajectory of our lives, whether positive or negative, will be significantly influenced by the number of good and bad habits running in the background. I knew building better habits, and getting rid of bad ones, was fundamental to every change I wanted to make. In my free time I quickly began organizing "Build Better Habits" meetups that were open to anyone. We met regularly and discussed different habit-formation strategies and books we were reading.

In the course of researching content for one of the meetups, I came across the work of Professor B.J. Fogg, who runs Stanford University's Behavior Design Lab. Desperate to learn more about behavior design and how it ties into habit formation, I reached out to him and completed a coaching certification and apprenticeship he was offering. He taught me a lot about the use of triggers to create habits and how they are an essential part of the habit loop: cue, routine, reward.

Around this time, I also spent many hours with author and psychologist Neil Fiore. Aside from the anti-procrastination techniques I shared in chapter 2 earlier, Neil got me hooked on the power of identity-based change, which I will cover in chapter 4. In short, Neil encouraged me to choose multiple identities that represented me at my best. These identities, he explained, could be chosen and used at will, and adapted to the situation at hand.

After working with Neil, I came across Brendon Burchard's work on high performance, previously mentioned. I quickly pored over his books, completed his coaching certification, and joined his mastermind. Brendon often talks about bringing intentionality into your day by thinking of three words or values that define you at your best across multiple domains of life. As a result, I began thinking of myself as fast, focused, and bold on the workfront, as well as decisive, inspiring, and reliable. Within my relationships I began thinking of myself as cool, calm, and present, while also being playful, fun, and full of laughter. The secret, Brendon advised, was to remind yourself of your values, within your different life domains, while also deciding the bold actions you would take to prove your greatness, on a daily basis.

Brian Johnson's similar perspective was also hugely influential to me. Brian also advocates defining a best-self identity across the domains of energy, work, and love, complete with a set of values and corresponding actions. During a call, Brain explained to me that he might become a professional athlete, energy-wise, on a given day—full of strength, confidence, and determination. He may also decide that completing a specific set of exercises would be the way he would prove he was stepping into that identity. Once again, this was something he did daily.

Pulling everything together, I had an idea. What if I set three alarms on my phone to trigger me: one to remind me I want to be healthy, one to remind me I want to be wealthy, and one to remind me I want to be a great husband and dad? I gave it a shot, and this simple action transformed my life. To this day I still have those three simple alarms going off every single day. They segment my day into the three domains of life, and each is powered by a best-self identity that means something to me. Collectively, they represent my *Dream Team*. Each identity gives me a goal to both shoot for and measure myself against. Sometimes, that self-management happens just before or in the moment, and I'm able to course correct. Sometimes, the alarm goes off after I do something I'm not proud of, and it prompts me to reflect.

At 6:30 a.m., the first alarm goes off: "World Fitness Champion."

The next rings at 9:00 a.m.: "World's Best Coach."

The last one goes off at 6:30 p.m., right as I'm arriving home for the day: "World's Best Husband and Father."

Am I actually the world's best at these things? No, I don't believe I am. But I sure want to be. We'll talk more about these three alarms and how to use them in your own life in Part 3. But for now, I just want you to know that setting these simple alarms is the single most important thing I have done to change my life and become a peak performer.

One way or another, you, too, will have a wake-up call. While you may never feel you're about to die 35,000 feet in the air, if you aren't proactive in these domains of life, you'll eventually have an experience that shakes you. Maybe you'll have a health scare, or be fired from your job, or lose a special relationship. Inevitably, an alarm will go off in your life and wake you up. So you might as well set them yourself first.

Before we get into the details of how to use the three alarms in your own life, we'll talk about the three key peak-performance habits I've learned over the years that have led to exponential growth. One of my superpowers has always been seeking out and connecting with experts. I have learned from some of the best in the world, and I'll share the most helpful things they've taught me in the next few chapters. The important thing is to apply these performance habits to all three domains of life.

PART 1 ACTION STEPS

1. Which peak performance traps do you identify with most: lack of intentionality, perfectionism, too much structure, procrastination, or hyperfocusing on a single domain?
2. Do you struggle with procrastination? If so, which of the four strategies can you incorporate into your life to tackle it: positive self-talk, focusing on starting, centering, and/or guilt-free play?
3. Are you the Workaholic, Martyr, or Health Nut? How do you think this has impacted the three domains of your life?
4. How might you better balance these domains?
5. When you think of yourself at your very best, what phrase or person comes to mind?
6. How might these identities differ across the health, work, and relationship fronts?

IPA: THREE KEYS TO PEAK PERFORMANCE

Part 2

OVERVIEW

Over the past twenty years, I have immersed myself in the field of peak performance: first in the wrong way, then in the right way. Before that plane emergency landed:

1. My professional achievements came with a lot of pain, and my health and relationships were a mess.
2. I really struggled with productivity, focus, and consistency in the structure-less environment entrepreneurs and leaders must thrive in.
3. I would manage to stick to my plans for a while, but then something unexpected would derail my progress.

However, since implementing what I will share in Part 2:

1. I show up more consistently as my best at work, I'm the healthiest I've ever been, and I've never done better in my role as a husband and father.
2. I've gone from battling bouts of procrastination to

becoming a super producer who can focus at will and generate incredible results with far less effort than before.

3. I've developed the mental toughness that enables me not just to survive when things don't go to plan, but to actually thrive in those situations.

I believe everyone can become extraordinary. Everyone can realize their full potential, and do it without the unhealthy hustle. We all want to improve, to become the very best we can be. Desire is not the problem. The issue is how. This next part addresses exactly that.

In Part 2, we're going to have you step into being your best by defining your identity. We're going to optimize you for action and by increasing your productivity. And we're going to prepare you for the unexpected by building your antifragility. Identity, productivity, and antifragility—IPA, like the beer, but better for you. IPA represents the powerful trio I've used to create all the results I listed above.

A word of warning before we begin: you may already know many of the principles to come. But knowing is not where the game is played. It's about translating knowledge into action. That's where the game is played.

So, let's take action. Let's begin!

4

IDENTITY-BASED CHANGE

After my near-death experience, I desperately wanted to change my health habits. When my wife said she was leaving me, I was motivated to change my relationship habits. And I have wanted to improve my work habits for as long as I can remember. I wanted to reach my full potential in all the areas of life that matter most. But to do this, I first had to evaluate who I thought I was.

In *Awaken Your Strongest Self*, Neil Fiore writes about being in his early forties and hitting a plateau in his skiing abilities. He was an intermediate skier and wanted to be much better, but he had just stopped improving.

One day, his ski instructor changed the script by saying, "For the rest of the day, you are Hans, the champion Swiss Alpine skier." I don't know if he actually chose the name Hans, but he basically told him to pretend he was a champion skier for the day. And something magical happened: Neil began to ski completely differently. He actually WAS skiing better. He was being Hans, not Neil.

Of course, he was still Neil—just a better-skiing Neil. He realized in that moment that it's much easier to switch to a new identity than it is to change yourself or a behavior. The capacity to ski that well was always inside him; he needed only to think about himself differently.

Most people focus on the things they want to change about themselves and the actions they want to take, but that can be overwhelming. It's actually easier to step into a new identity than it is to try to create new habits and behaviors in a vacuum.

As you change your identity, your behaviors and habits change, too.

BEHAVIOR FOLLOWS IDENTITY

In *Atomic Habits*, bestselling author James Clear writes about the etymology of the word *identity*: it is made up of two words meaning "repeated beingness." This is how habits happen: by repeatedly assuming a new identity. It is also the difference between saying, "I want to stop procrastinating" and "I want to be a person who does not procrastinate."

When I worked with Neil, I wanted to do just that: redefine myself as someone who doesn't procrastinate. I wanted to be a person who is focused, creative, and able to work distraction-free for whatever time is required. That, I thought, was the strongest, most heroic version of me, and it was the identity I desired.

This thought process is often referred to as identity-based change, and is the most powerful way to change behavior and build healthy habits that last a lifetime.

Once you assume a new identity, you start behaving like this heroic version of yourself. As Nassim Taleb writes in *Fooled by Randomness*, "Heroes are heroes because they are heroic in behavior, not because they won or lost." The more you repeat a behavior, the more you become the identity associated with it. Behaviors reinforce the identity we want, and our chosen identity guides our behaviors. It's a virtuous cycle, although identity should come first —or at least it's much easier when it does.

In my work with Neil, I wrote out a description of my best-self identity. It was the equivalent of "Hans" on the ski slope. I had also done a lot of work on identity and values from a company point of view, with Chilango, the Mexican restaurant chain I had co-founded. The one-word distillation of Chilango's identity was "vibrancy," and the company's values were "principled, offbeat, fun, and determined." Marrying these ideas with some of the previously mentioned influences, I decided to define one identity for each of the three domains of life, with a corresponding set of values that would define how that best-self version of me would act and behave.

In health, the best version of me, the "World Fitness Champion," is relentless, pain-seeking, and varied in approach because that's what I associate with world-class fitness. In my work as a coach, or shall I say the "World's Best Coach," my best self is decisive, inspiring, and reliable. And in my relationships, as the "World's Best Husband & Father," I'm playful, loving, and full of laughter. Just as a set of values helps a company and its culture behave in line with its identity, my personal values within each domain of life help me act and behave in line with each domain's identity.

In Part 3, I'll explain how I set three alarms that go off every day and continually reinforce these identities and values.

MAKING A NEW IDENTITY STICK

It's one thing to set an intention to change, and quite another to believe it so powerfully that it influences your actions and behaviors. In my experience, you have to create some kind of proof for yourself to really make a new identity stick.

After I had defined what my best identity was in each of the three domains, I wanted to provide evidence that I was stepping into these identities on a daily basis. If these identities represented the champion version of me, I needed something to prove I was being who I said I wanted to be. So I created a concept called "champion proofs," similar to a practice Brian Johnson advocates, whereby you choose the number-one thing you could do each day to evidence you at your best.

Each day, I ask myself what single thing I could do to prove I'm the champion version of myself in each area of life that matters most. Each day could be different. As I go through the segments of my day, I pick one thing to accomplish within each domain as proof that I'm becoming a better me. In the gym, it may be that I'd like to burn 500 calories or do a certain number of sets and repetitions on the leg press. At work, maybe I set out to complete my content calendar or finish a presentation. And in my relationships, I could decide to play a video game with my son or have coffee with my wife or a friend. Whatever makes the most sense in each area of life within the context of that day.

A helpful exercise to choose the right "champion proofs" is to spend a few minutes visualizing your day. Review your schedule, and actually picture yourself moving through your day and the actions that your best self would take. This will help you pick your one action item for each identity. You might look at a work day full of meetings and realize that there is one meeting that is significantly more important than the others. So you decide to carve out some extra preparation time to ensure you show up as your absolute best. On the health front, you might spot a potentially dangerous lunch appointment and decide in advance that you will stick to your healthy eating plan as your champion proof. And on the relationship front, you might simply decide to call a friend or family member as your action item for the day. Champion proofs let you rack up small wins, day after day, to prove you're stepping into the person you're capable of being.

Choosing your champion proofs at the start of the day also works well with the three alarms. When each alarm goes off, they not only remind me of my best-self identity for that domain, but they also prompt me to check in with my champion proof for that segment of my day. That said, sometimes the alarm simply changes the way I'm walking into work or home, giving me the shake-up I need if I'm not already in the right state of mind.

When you pick a champion proof, you become very intentional about the tangible things you could do in a day to prove you're stepping into a better you. I keep my identities and values pretty static, while the actions I take each day as champion proofs might differ.

WHAT TO DO WHEN WE FAIL

There will always be things throughout the day that come up and get in your way. As Mike Tyson once said, "Everyone has a plan until they get punched in the mouth." But when you have taken the time to define what your best looks like, even when your day gets derailed, you're much more likely to course correct and make better decisions.

You might get in an argument with your spouse and say something you regret, but then quickly apologize. Maybe you'll lose your cool with your children, but regain your composure. At work, you may be tempted to quit early on a project or put something off, but then remind yourself to be reliable for others. These course corrections are far more likely if you've defined what best looks like. Suddenly, when you're off target, it becomes painfully obvious.

Over time, you'll notice that you're not falling as hard, or you'll catch yourself in the moment. You will more consistently live up to the best version of you. During your morning visualization, you could even imagine things going wrong in order to plan how you would react, from the vantage point of you at your best

Most people aspire to become their best selves some time in the future, but peak performers define what "best" looks like right now and start behaving from that identity today. Closing the gap between your current self and best self is about continually getting better, little by little, and bouncing back more quickly from your mistakes.

Imagine your best self as a straight, horizontal line on a chart. The current you sits somewhere below that line. Each day you inch closer, and sometimes fall back, but you continue in a general upward trend. As your identity guides your behavior, and your behavior reinforces your identity, you become a better you. Over time, the gap between your current self and your best self narrows.

5

PRODUCTIVITY PLANNING

If you're anything like me, you've looked in the mirror plenty of times and thought you should be further along than you were. Perhaps you don't feel like there is enough time in the day to do the work that matters most.

But there is a window of opportunity to change the trajectory of your life. Why take years to do what can be done in months, or maybe never do the things you've always dreamed of doing? It's possible to produce far more than you realize. But you can't reach your full potential without mastering the art of getting the right things done with the least amount of effort. That is true productivity.

With a little bit of research, you'll find endless tips on how to become more productive. I can't cover everything, but I will share with you what I've found to deliver the best results for both me and my clients.

Many people feel they lack willpower, self-discipline, or focus. But most of the time, they just need some simple strategies to help them be more productive. Learning to work smarter, not harder, is one of the main ways I have increased my performance and achieved the things I want.

We're going to break down productivity in two parts: planning and execution. Before you sit down to work and accomplish everything you set out to do, you have to make a plan. Here are the three ways I plan to be productive before I actually sit down and begin.

DESIGN YOUR DAY

One of the secrets to performing at a peak level is to string together as many winning days as possible. Jerry Seinfeld used to hang a year-at-a-glance calendar on his wall every January. Every day that he wrote new material, he would put a big red X on that day's square. The goal was simple: don't break the chain.

So how do we create as many winning days as possible? We start by designing powerful routines into our days. Every day is different, but having a construct of what an ideal day looks like is incredibly helpful. If you want to be more productive, you need to literally design productivity into your day.

Most people talk about morning routines, but a great day begins the night before with an evening routine and a great night's sleep. Without an evening routine, you'll have difficulty maintaining a morning routine for very long.

My work day ends with a shutdown appointment, inspired by Cal Newport's book *Deep Work*. I do a final sweep of my to-do list and email and check my calendar for the next day. I choose my top three things to accomplish the following day, and then schedule them into my calendar as appointments with myself. Then, I shut down. No more work. No more replaying conversations in my head, thinking about emails I need to write, or wondering what I should do tomorrow. As a result I'm able to head home and be fully present with my family.

The next part of my evening routine is a digital sunset. This is an additional alarm that goes off one hour before bed (such that I can get eight hours of sleep) to remind me to shut off the electronics. When that alarm goes off, I shut everything down—phone, TV, and computer. In *Why We Sleep*, Matthew Walker shares the shocking statistic that our devices can reduce the production of the sleep-inducing hormone melatonin by up to 50%. Without enough melatonin in the body, you'll find it difficult to sleep a full eight hours, and even if you do, it's not likely to be as deep and restorative as it should.

Why does artificial light suppress melatonin production? It begins with the pea-sized pineal gland that sits at the center of our brain. Artificial light comes through our eyes and is picked up by this gland. As we've evolved to sleep at night, rather than during the day, the pineal gland suppresses production of melatonin when it detects light, including the light from your electronic devices, thinking that it's still daytime.

What's the ultimate goal of a digital sunset? Ensuring that you get the recommended eight hours of sleep. If you don't get a good night's sleep, you won't be able to focus as well, and you will be more prone to irritation and anxiety, which will destroy your productivity. And those are only the short-term consequences. In the long term, sleep deprivation has been linked to increased risk of cardiovascular disease, cancer, and mental illness. That's a trifecta that we don't want to mess with.

Some people do have a gene that allows them to thrive on less than eight hours of sleep, but as Walker points out, you're more likely to be struck by lightning than to have this gene. So you probably need eight hours, too. It's not about surviving with less; it's about thriving with more.

Having a morning routine is just as important as having an evening routine, but I bet you knew that already, as they're much more fun to talk about. There is not one perfect way to start your morning. The important thing is that you find what works for you. My morning routine takes about sixty minutes.

A perfect day for me begins with journaling, looking at the day ahead, and picking my champion proofs for each of my three best-self identities. I may write a statement or two to affirm myself. This serves to remind me of my strength, resilience, and brilliance. We all have that within us, by the way—you just need to remind yourself.

Then I visualize being my best self in each domain in the context of that day. I anticipate where the day may go wrong, likely challenges, negative thoughts, or procrastination, and how I'll deal with each.

Next up for me is meditation. I use a simple breathing meditation, nothing fancy. I sit in a relaxed, upright position, close my eyes, and begin taking some deep breaths, similar to the centering exercise I use when I'm tempted to procrastinate. I do this for ten minutes.

Next, I will read for about twenty minutes. I love reading and often have trouble fitting it into my schedule. The solution I've found is to frontload it to make sure it gets done.

I close out my morning routine with exercise. Numerous studies have confirmed that long-term exercise can not only benefit our bodies physically, but also fight depression and significantly boost our moods equivalent in strength to an antidepressant. I often ask my coaching clients, "When would you like to take your antidepressant—at the start of the day to benefit from that mood boost, or at the end of your day before you go to sleep?" Nine times out of ten, clients say at the start of their day.

You can implement my exact morning routine or just parts of it. You can do them in the same order or switch them up. The point is that you develop something that works for you. Aim for a concrete structure that you don't need to think about. You'll be amazed at how this sets you up for success each day.

If it feels overwhelming to think of designing every day like this, start with the digital sunset. Then add in other things as you become more consistent. Add new puzzle pieces after you have a few weeks of solid performance.

Ending and starting my days with powerful routines led to a significant increase in my productivity and my number of "winning days."

CREATIVE BEFORE REACTIVE

After exercise, I begin my work. Having outlined my three priorities the night before and reviewed them when I woke up, I don't start by dipping into my inbox, looking at my calendar, or doing other things that will put me in reactive mode. Being reactive first thing in the day feels like getting dropped into a pinball machine and bouncing from one person's agenda to the next.

Brian Johnson says, "Always be creative before reactive." I love that. In the first hour of your day, don't hop on social media or start responding to emails. Try to do something creative instead of reactive. What should you do? One of your top three priorities for the day, chosen as part of your shutdown ritual the day before, is the perfect place to start.

Another way to think of being creative before reactive is being a maker versus a manager. It's simple: a maker makes things, and a manager manages things. I try to divide my time this way by implementing maker mornings and manager afternoons. I keep my mornings free from meetings or interacting with others so I can put forth my best creative thinking and work, when my energy is also at its highest. I recommend taking frequent breaks during creative time; otherwise, you may feel your energy and focus begin to wane. I work in hour-long blocks of time, setting a timer for fifty minutes to prompt a ten-minute break after each period of work. Then my afternoons are used for manager time or simply interacting with others.

Since your energy is generally highest when you first wake up, do the most cognitively demanding things first, when your focus, concentration, and willpower are all at their strongest. I think of people like batteries. We start off at 100% charged, and ideally we'd stay that way throughout the day. But of course, that's not what batteries do. They drain, and so do you.

Throughout the day, your energy wanes, and by the afternoon, you might be closer to 50%. Use your afternoons for internal and external meetings, administrative and executive tasks, and handling email. One of the reasons I like to interact with people in the afternoon is to help me keep my energy up. If there are three of us working on a project, and we're each at 33% charged, then combined we're just about 100%. I know it's not very scientific, but it's a fun way I like to think about it.

MASSIVE GOALS = MASSIVE RESULTS

While we continuously optimize our productivity, we still need something to be productive "toward." When I was helping build Skype, our tagline was "The Whole World Can Talk for Free." It created a revolutionary spirit inside the company as we all rowed in sync, knowing we were doing the world good by connecting people who couldn't otherwise speak, increasing the frequency of their communication, or simply adding the video element that we now take for granted. Having such a massive goal inspired massive action, which led to massive results—including our sale to eBay for $4 billion.

I've noticed time and again that when I commit to a huge goal, even though I don't think I will be able to achieve it, somehow it still gets done.

We develop the skills we need, when we need them, by just going for it. In his book *The Big Leap*, Gay Hendricks says that the moment you commit and take that step forward, a bridge appears underneath your feet. Whenever I have set big goals, I have found and connected to all of the expertise I needed to achieve them.

But it's not magic. One of my favorite quotes is from John Burroughs: "Leap, and the net will appear." Truth be told, the "net" isn't providence or God saving your butt because you leapt. What really happens is you're weaving the net as you fall. It doesn't appear out of nowhere. When you make that decision to take action against something that scares and excites you at the same time, the net appears in the form of the various resources you gather—be they money, people, or opportunities. When you put the pressure on yourself to go make things happen, you'll be surprised by how often they do. Necessity truly is the mother of invention.

Setting massive goals for you and your business is a next-level productivity driver for a variety of reasons:

1. It forces us to commit before we're ready. Rather than waiting for things to be just right, which they never are, we are pushed to get going.
2. It enables us to dream big—and when we dream big, we get excited. We are measurably more productive working on something that excites us.
3. It makes us hyper-aware of time. When we go big, we know that every second counts. We're more compelled to give our very best, every single day.
4. It forces us to take commensurate action. Rather than

berate ourselves for not acting boldly or quickly enough day after day, massive goals leave us no choice.

5. Lastly, massive goals prompt us to get real with ourselves and confront our deficiencies.

Winning "CEO of the Year" was a perfect example. What started as an idea to improve my leadership abilities changed into an epic quest to become a significantly better leader. The mere pursuit of the goal prompted me to take action I wouldn't have otherwise considered. I reached out to interview various CEOs to understand what drove their success. I sought feedback more often from my team and advisors. I read countless books on leadership and peak performance. And I began tracking key behaviors to ensure I was making progress; behaviors I now train up in clients eager to upgrade their leadership skills.

Growing up, my parents used to say, "Shoot for the moon, and even if you miss, you'll still land among the stars." I knew that even if I didn't win, I would learn so much along the way, and that alone would be worth it. While I did end up winning that award, that wasn't the real prize. The real prize was who I had to become to win it, all driven by shooting for a goal that initially seemed out of reach.

6

PRODUCTIVITY EXECUTION

Productivity isn't just about planning; it's also about execution. To be truly productive, you have to be able to implement the plan you've made. But far too often, we focus on the wrong tasks and end up wasting time and energy. Management guru Peter Drucker famously said, "There is nothing so useless as doing efficiently that which should not be done at all."

80/20 FOCUS

The Pareto Principle, or what's often called The 80/20 Rule, states that roughly 80% of the effects come from 20% of the causes. This was one of the most important concepts drilled into my head at McKinsey & Company. Working with CEOs and executives of the world's largest companies, part of our role was to help them focus on what mattered most. And more often than not, it was a few vital factors that drove most of the results.

For a period of time, I began looking for 80/20 opportunities throughout my day, keen to develop the habit of doing things more quickly. I struck up an accountability partnership with a friend, in which every day we would report to one another one thing we had "80/20ed" that day. An example where we had achieved 80% of the result with only 20% of the effort. Sometimes 80/20 thinking prompts you to uncover an easier path. Not all tasks or actions are created equal, and the vital few will always matter more than the trivial many.

When I found myself in a rut, I began asking myself how I was making things too difficult. Let things flow, and ask yourself how they could be easier. As Gary Keller writes in *The One Thing*, before beginning a project or task, always ask yourself, "What's the one thing I could do such that by doing it everything else becomes easier or unnecessary?" Just because things are hard doesn't make them important or efficient. Make things as easy for yourself as you can.

Other times, 80/20 thinking prompted me to do things more quickly. I used to take ages to send out notes following important strategic meetings, because I wrote them so meticulously. Then one day, I sat down to type a set of notes and realized I needed to be on a call in twenty-one minutes. I thought to myself, *Let me see if I can type up these notes and press send before 6:00 p.m.* So I typed up the notes and sent them out in those twenty-one minutes. They didn't cover absolutely everything, but it was 80% of the results for 20% of the effort.

Dan Sullivan presents another take on the 80/20 rule in *The 80% Approach*, which advocates using the 80/20 principle several times on a single piece of work. A simplified explanation is this: go over a task once, giving it 80% effort. This is often enough, and you can move on to the next task. Or you can do another 80/20 round, giving an 80% effort on the 20% that remains. Two rounds of 80/20 effort in this way yields what I like to call "the 96% solution." It's not 100%, but it's pretty damn close. And you have the added benefit of not aiming for perfection each time.

I recently did this with a colleague I'm working with to create a content calendar for my site. I quickly put together fifty-two weeks of content ideas. He took a look at it, 80/20ed it, and sent me the feedback. Within two rounds, we had created the 96% solution for our content calendar. Will the rest of the world notice that 4% is missing? No. Even I'm not sure I could tell you how to improve it. Really good is good enough.

One of my favorite applications of the 80/20 rule was at Chilango. When we first started, we knew that there were many factors that drove guest satisfaction. There's the interior, the staff, the customer service, etc. But we decided that the 20% of the equation that would drive 80% of the results was the food. And within the food, we did another 80/20 evaluation. What was really important to us was flavor. It's all well and good where the food is sourced and how it's prepared, but if it tastes awful, source and prep don't matter. We believed people were paying for flavor when they purchased from Chilango.

With flavor in the crosshairs, my business partner and I ate our way through Mexico and some of America's largest Mexican communities. We picked up recipes from street vendors and high-end chefs. Once, we even placed an ad offering $500 to whoever could supply us with the best slow-cooked pork recipe. A chef from Cleveland replied. I hopped on a plane and flew to the United States. The pork was bursting with flavor, exactly as promised, and I gave him $500 cash on the spot.

But we didn't stop with recipes as we 80/20ed flavor. Next, we asked what 20% of the ingredients drove 80% of the flavor in the recipes that mattered most. All of that maniacal 80/20 focus led us to form relationships with farmers in Mexico so we could get the absolute best quality and flavor in certain ingredients. To this day, Chilango receives these key ingredients directly from Mexico.

I have become so obsessed with 80/20ing things in my life that I use it even in my health and relationships. Before I started applying the Pareto Principle, I researched many different health plans and fitness routines. I burned a lot of time doing that. When it comes to health, there are only a few items you need to do to produce 80% of the results you want. These are the 20%: get eight hours of sleep, eat well, and work out. It's not complicated, but it's not easy, either. In *Why We Sleep*, Walker writes that the bridge from despair to hope is often a good night's sleep. I've certainly felt that many times along the way. When things feel off or I'm down, I usually just need a good night's sleep.

Author and activist Michael Pollan says, "Eat food, not too much, mostly plants." That's the 80/20 of diet. There are tons of different diet and lifestyle plans out there. But if you eat real, non-processed food, not too much, and mostly plants, you're doing it right. It doesn't matter whether you do keto, paleo, or South Beach—they all basically boil down to that.

When I decided to 80/20 my marriage, I wanted to pick one proactive thing and one reactive thing to work on. I asked my wife, "What is just one thing I could do better, more often, or more consistently that would improve our relationship?" I have actually suggested this to people before, and they sometimes recoil at the thought. The biggest inhibition to doing this is that most people are afraid to hear the answer. We don't like hearing what we're doing wrong, or hearing something about us that isn't as great as we thought. By asking for it, you're acknowledging it and putting your ass on the line. I strongly suggest you try it. And do it as a leader, too. Ask your employees the same question: "What could I work on? What could I do to make your job easier?" You'll learn so much from it, and it will make you a better person.

My wife's answer was that she just wanted to spend more time together without expectation or agenda. In *Rhythm of Life*, Matthew Kelly shares his take on "quality time." He says you don't achieve quality time with someone by looking for it. You achieve it by having blocks of "carefree timelessness," within which quality time can spontaneously emerge—whether it's laughter, an unexpected conversation, or a bit of encouragement. Pressuring yourself to find quality time makes you less likely to find it. I think this is an especially helpful concept for men. Before Gisele asked me to simply spend time with her, without expectation, I typically thought, "Okay, what are we going to do so I can tick the quality time box?" Whereas she was thinking about it very differently. She wanted to spend a longer period of time together with no agenda, and allow quality time to happen on its own.

I also asked my fourteen-year-old son what I could do to improve our relationship, and he said he'd like to go on more adventures together. So we co-created an adventure list of things we wanted to do together over the following three years. It included things like indoor skydiving, bungee jumping, and rock climbing. When I asked my six-year-old son, he said he just wanted to play together more. Now that I have these answers, I can be actively working on our relationships in a way that means the most to them.

That's how I proactively zeroed in on the 20% of things that could create 80% of the improvement in my relationships. You can also use the 80/20 principle to react better in your relationships. Although our family members are without doubt our "loved ones," our partners, spouses, or children can still trigger the worst in us. It may be a certain thing they tend to say or do, or it could be their own reaction to a situation. We can acquire half of the improvement we seek in our relationships simply by reacting better to those around us. We're often so preoccupied with what we could do proactively that we miss the reactive side of the coin.

What I mean is, focus on that one pet peeve of yours. What does your partner, spouse, or child do that perhaps annoys you? Pick one thing that they do, and commit to practicing patience. Become aware of what it is, identify it, and then deliberately pause when it happens such that you don't react right away. We will cover the power of "the pause" in greater detail in chapter 7, but it's essentially giving yourself a moment to choose the best response rather than go into a default emotional, suboptimal response. This moment or pause could come in the form of a deep breath, a silent count to three, or a simple break from the situation. Anything that affords us the ability to create a tiny bit of space between whatever is triggering us and how we respond.

One of Stephen Covey's favorite concepts was the notion that our freedom lies within that space between stimulus and response. Just about anything imaginable could happen to us during the course of life, but we always can choose how we want to respond. I have my coaching clients think about each of their family members and identify the one thing they do that typically triggers a negative reaction or response from them. We typically don't perceive our reactions as a path to improving our relationships, but they are, as mentioned, often half the battle. Simply react better to the things that irritate you and your relationships will improve. You don't even need to let your family members in on the game. Just commit on your own to knowing what typically triggers you, pause when it happens, and choose your best response. Think of how the wisest version of you, the ninety-five year old version of you, would respond.

People are often equally resistant to this practice because it is another act of vulnerability. It's a concession of their right to complain or be unhappy. But this is how we grow. In *The Big Leap*, Gay Hendricks talks about the 200% relationship. No matter what has happened before a certain point, you take 100% of the responsibility for why the relationship is the way it is, and you take 100% of the responsibility for improving it.

The beautiful thing about the 80/20 principle is that it reduces the set of actions you could take down to the most important, meaningful ones. It's an incredible simplification. I encourage you to begin applying this idea wherever you can.

I even 80/20ed the preparation of my wedding speech. I am American and Norwegian, and my wife is Brazilian. When we got engaged, I promised her whole family that I would give my wedding speech in Portuguese. The only problem was, I didn't speak Portuguese. So I researched rapid language-acquisition methods in search of the 20% of techniques that would create 80% of the benefit. In the process, I networked my way to some of the most accomplished, self-taught polyglots in the world, including Idahosa Ness and Olly Richards.

Idahosa suggested I learn to rap first because rap is faster than speech. If you can replicate and understand rap, he explained, conversation sounds slow in comparison. So I had a blast learning to rap in Portuguese, going from a zero to intermediate level in the language in less than a year. I also nailed the speech, by the way. There is literally nothing you can't 80/20.

ADD 13 WEEKS TO YOUR LIFE PER YEAR

One of the most important things I learned about improving my productivity was the power of single-tasking. I read in *The ONE Thing* that researchers estimate 28% of the average work day is lost to task switching. This is because of the inefficiency of jumping from one thing to another and reorienting yourself each time with what you were originally doing when you return to it. It massively slows down your task-completion rate.

The statistic is far more alarming if we extrapolate the consequences. Take 28% of each work day, forty-six weeks a year (assuming a generous six weeks of vacation). Forty-six weeks times a 28% loss equates to thirteen weeks a year lost to task switching. That's an entire calendar quarter!

So, of course, the average person feels overworked and unproductive. They're playing with only three-quarters in their year instead of four. What could you do with an extra quarter?

If you master the habit of single-tasking and aren't constantly distracted throughout your work day, especially during your creative time, you can reclaim those thirteen weeks. Think of all you could get done! Over a ten-year period, that's another two and a half years of your life. Over a career of forty years, you'll add a whole extra decade. What could you do with an extra decade?

What you use those extra weeks and years for is up to you. Perhaps you want to use them to increase your output and accomplish more than the average person. Maybe you want to use single-tasking to get your work done in a shorter amount of time and use the rest to do other things you enjoy. People are running around feeling like they don't have enough time to get everything done, and it's because they're playing with only three quarters of the year. How advantageous would it be if you could suddenly be playing the game of life with all four quarters? That's the power of single-tasking.

How do you develop the habit of single-tasking? Start with a simple timesheet. Simply note every activity you perform throughout the day with a start time, an end time, and your total minutes. The secret here is to record literally everything. Thirteen minutes spent working on a presentation. Five minutes spent grabbing a coffee. Eleven minutes spent in your inbox. Seventeen minutes spent "researching" that irresistible idea that just popped in your head. Six minutes spent answering that phone call.

As you record each and every task you engage in, you'll become more and more aware of just how often you switch tasks, as well as how often you're switching to something rather meaningless. Over time you'll think twice about having to record that you randomly surfed Facebook for twenty-four minutes, for example.

Once you've developed an awareness of where your time goes, how often you switch from one task to the next, and your typical distractions, it's time to start expanding your ability to work without interruption, and distraction-free! Begin by optimizing your environment. Leave your phone in another room when trying to complete a block of focused work. Shut off all notifications, close down any tabs or documents not needed for the work at hand, and try working in full screen mode. At first you may only achieve fifteen minutes of uninterrupted work, as will be evidenced by your timesheet. But over time, you will grow those focused blocks of time to thirty minutes, fifty minutes, and so on. Soon, the length of your time sheets will shorten as you focus on the task at hand for longer and longer, resulting in fewer entries per day. And as your time sheets shorten, the weeks you will reclaim will grow.

MEASURE AND MONITOR

What gets measured, gets done. And when it comes to measurement, I like to think about milestone-related goals, peak performance routines, and regular reviews. For example, while in pursuit of the CEO award, a milestone goal for me, I noted decisiveness and reliability as critical behaviors. So at the end of each day, I reflected on how decisive and reliable I had been in my business and with my employees. If I had made a decision particularly quickly, I noted that. If I had taken too long on a decision, or behaved too ambiguously, I noted that as well. Similarly, if I was quick to do what I had promised and had acted dependably, I rated myself high in reliability. If I was late on a task or didn't properly follow through, I scored myself negatively. In practice, this meant simply noting my positives and negatives in decisiveness and reliability on a daily basis.

Over the years, I've noted a set of five factors that significantly improve my productivity. Together they form my peak-performance routine:

1. Getting eight hours of sleep.
2. Completing ninety minutes of high-quality, focused, distraction-free work by 7:30 a.m.
3. Completing at least twenty minutes of moderate exercise by 8:30 a.m.
4. Shutting down my day by 6:30 p.m.
5. Practicing a digital sunset by 8:30 p.m.

I don't always do all five of these things, but when I do, I typically have a winning day. I've set up a very simple checklist where I track these five factors daily. The more tick marks I see, the better.

Our lives and experiences are overflowing with data. Valuable diamonds are just waiting to be mined. Sensing the value in intentional reflection, I began performing quarterly reviews of my professional and personal life. I noted all of the areas in which I made good decisions and showed up at my best self, and the moments where I faltered and could have done better. I gained a tremendous amount of self awareness that I had never experienced before. I learned to be brutally honest with myself and not convince myself things were better than they were.

At the end of each quarter, I made a list of every area where I succeeded and failed, insights I had, and actions I could take. Just this simple activity yielded huge results for me.

When it comes to regular reviews, the real game-changer is the weekly review. I can't underscore enough how important and valuable it is to review the week that's just past, and set up your coming week for success. You'll find all sorts of planners on the market, and I highly encourage you to find the one that suits you best, and put it to diligent use.

I typically use one hour to complete my weekly review on a Sunday. Some of my coaching clients prefer doing their review on a Friday afternoon instead. During my review I note the following:

- My big wins, or proudest accomplishments, for the week
- My performance against the Top 3 objectives I had chosen for the week
- What went well and what didn't, generally speaking
- My appointments for the week ahead
- The Top 3 objectives for the week ahead
- Where and when I will complete next week's Top 3

Last but not least is my daily review, which is contained within the shutdown ritual that I mentioned earlier as part of my evening routine.

As we discussed in Part 1, people underestimate the power of intentionality. Purposeful reviews create huge benefits.

SAMPLE QUARTERLY REVIEW SUMMARY

Successes

1. Maintained peak-performance habits
2. Stabilized the company and team
3. Raised funds for next phase of growth
4. Upgraded company-wide marketing
5. Launched leadership development program

Failures

1. Worked too much, felt worn out
2. Failed to follow-up on marketing project on time
3. Missed language learning goals in Portuguese
4. Extended two project deadlines unnecessarily
5. Didn't spend sufficient time with family and friends

Insights

1. Perfectionism is a big development opportunity
2. Reading should be scheduled into the day
3. The mind needs to be trained as much as the body
4. Weekly reviews must result in new weekly commitments
5. I want to become world-class at peak performance

Actions

1. Determine what are the non-negotiables in my life
2. Increase output with a color-coded master calendar
3. Bring the joy/be more intentional
4. Hire a virtual assistant
5. Create a weekly accountability checklist

7

ANTIFRAGILITY: STRESS BUILDS STRENGTH

Despite all our identity and productivity improvements, things will still not go to plan. Handling setbacks is a natural part of life and work, especially for an entrepreneur. Entrepreneurial resilience is a popular topic in the self-development and start-up spaces. But to become a peak performer, you need something more than resilience—you need antifragility.

My life changed when I read *Antifragile* by Nassim Taleb. Antifragility represents the realm beyond resilience. Resilient people survive stress and stay the same, while antifragile people thrive specifically *because* of the stress. They don't stay the same; they come out stronger.

I am lucky enough to count some former US Special Forces operatives among my coaching clients. These men are masters of antifragility, and there is quite a lot we can learn from them. They don't see stress as something just to survive, but also as a benefit, as an opportunity for growth. They lean into discomfort, welcome it even. They're trained to expect the unexpected and still deliver with excellence.

Just as elite warriors are trained to run toward the sound of gunfire, we, too, must train ourselves to step into fear, hardship, and uncertainty. Discomfort then transforms from something to be avoided into a magnetic force that beckons our call. Moments of unease suddenly become signposts that say, "Step in this direction." As the great Roman emperor Marcus Aurelius put it, "The impediment to action advances action. What stands in the way becomes the way."

Even your body has something to teach you about antifragility, and it practices it all the time. In small doses, UV radiation repairs tissue and generates vitamin D, which is essential for every single cell in your body. Exposure to germs and bacteria builds up your immunity. Stressing a muscle by working out causes it to grow. In all of these ways, your body isn't just surviving a stressor (radiation, germs, overload), but using it to grow stronger. It's transforming stress into strength.

I'm particularly interested in the mental side of antifragility since my body is more fragile than most. I have a condition called Ehlers-Danlos Syndrome, type 3. It's a collagen disorder that causes a lot of hypermobility in all of my joints. They injure easily, and I have to be very careful in everything I do. I wasn't diagnosed until I was forty years old and had dealt with all kinds of pain and injuries my whole life, never knowing why I was so injury prone. I have torn ligaments in both of my ankles, fractured the cartilage in my knee cap down to the boney plate, sprained an ACL, torn ligaments off my shoulder socket, herniated a disc in my lower back, fractured a vertebrae, and torn the labrum within my left hip. I have had five surgeries on my left shoulder alone.

I also suffer from a condition called spondylolisthesis, which means the top half of my body is no longer appropriately attached to the bottom half via the vertebral column. If it gets much worse, I'll have to have my spine fused. Multiple times, my wife has seen me in so much pain that I was in tears. As I sit here writing this very moment, I can feel the pain in my right knee, which first began about three years ago and has never completely healed.

Staying in the antifragility mindset can be quite hard when my body actually feels very fragile. But the same antifragility concepts that apply to our bodies also apply to our minds. I use my challenging physical circumstances to strengthen myself mentally. I've come to embrace my daily pains, and in so doing, I have been set free.

What follows is a collection of tools, frames, and concepts to help you step into the pain that accompanies reaching your full potential.

IT'S NOT STRESS, IT'S YOU

I'd like you to think of three groups of people. The first group lives a relatively stress-free life. The second group experiences stress and views it positively. The final group experiences stress and views it negatively. Which group do you think lives the longest? It's the second group. The problem isn't stress. It's you.

We need to reframe stress in a positive way. With this in mind, I like to envision life as one big mental gym. Every moment of adversity, unexpected event, or thing that doesn't go our way can suddenly become an exercise in the gym of life. You don't become physically stronger by going to the gym one time. You have to go regularly and get your reps in. So it is with antifragility. Every challenge can become an opportunity for growth if you choose to see it that way.

In his personal journal, Aurelius wrote, "When force of circumstance upsets your equanimity, lose no time in recovering your self-control, and do not remain out of tune longer than you can help. Habitual recurrence to the harmony will increase your mastery of it." He was reminding himself that he would be knocked down in life, and that he must stand back up and regain his composure as quickly as possible. The more he bounced back, the better he would become at it.

I've already said it once in this book, but because it is one of my favorite proverbs, it bears repeating: *Fall down seven times, stand up eight.* Pursuing a stress-free life should not be your goal. Your goal should be to step into discomfort and challenge, expecting stressors as a natural part of that, and to use those to make you stronger and better.

Author Kelly McGonigal is a health psychologist at Stanford University. In her book *The Upside of Stress,* she explains that "the best way to manage stress isn't to reduce or avoid it, but rather to rethink and even embrace it." It is indeed our perception of stress that will determine its impact.

McGonigal's research demonstrates that an antifragile mindset actually enhances performance and productivity. A person with this mindset believes that stress improves health and vitality, while also facilitating learning and growth. They believe the effects of stress are positive, and a force to be utilized. A person with an antifragile mindset is "more likely to view stressful situations as a challenge, not an overwhelming problem."

Most people don't believe any of the above. They view stress negatively, and stressful situations as threatening.

The key, therefore, is seeing stress as a force for good, as something you both expect and seek to embrace. McGonigal writes, "Psychologists found that the most important factor in determining your response to pressure is how you think about your ability to handle it."

So how do we equip ourselves to respond to stress positively? Here are some of my favorite mindset shifts:

- Acknowledge your personal strengths—perhaps you're nervous about stepping out on to stage, despite having spoken to groups of people many times before.
- Imagine the support of your loved ones—as if you partner, spouse, or children were at your side, enthusiastically encouraging you to step ahead.
- Remember times in the past when you overcame similar challenges—you may not have experienced that exact same situation before, but you have most certainly thrived through a similar level of challenge.
- Summon the most courageous version of yourself, and then follow your own advice—we often find it's easier to give advice to others than follow our own, so bring this outside wisdom into the picture.

In working on both myself and with clients, I find the last point, summoning your most courageous self, to be the most powerful. Within us all lies a wise presence, unconditioned by past experiences. When faced with fear, uncertainty, and discomfort, summon this presence instead of trying to handle everything alone.

The approach is simple. When faced with a stressful situation, take a moment to pause. Close your eyes and imagine the most courageous you standing right there next to you. Ask that version of you how best to tackle or process the stress at hand. Listen for the response, and then follow the orders.

And on that note, let's delve further into the art of the pause.

THE PAUSE

In 1963, the American psychologist Rollo May wrote in "Freedom and Responsibility Re-Examined" that "human freedom involves our capacity to pause between stimulus and response and, in that pause, to choose the one response toward which we wish to throw our weight. The capacity to create ourselves, based upon this freedom, is inseparable from consciousness or self-awareness."

Stephen Covey, most likely influenced by May's article, wrote, "Between stimulus and response, there is a space. In that space is our power to choose our response. In our response lies our growth and our freedom."

These concepts are incredibly powerful from an antifragility point of view, as they transform stress into an opportunity to build strength. As we now appreciate, it's not stress that we should avoid, but our negative view of it, and our negative response to it.

Reframing stress within "the pause" is one of the simplest yet most powerful ways to become antifragile.

When something happens that triggers us, it's easy to believe that our emotional response is fused to it, that it's a natural reaction that can't be helped. But this isn't true. You have more control than you think.

Sometimes the thing that triggers you is obvious: someone cuts you off in traffic, a partner says something hurtful, or your child breaks an expensive vase. But triggers can also include things like receiving a bad report at work, a team member not following instructions, or just intrusive thoughts that remind you *again* of all the things you have to worry about. The reaction that follows often occurs without thought, and it's often a sub-optimal, fragile response. In other words, it's usually not the response your best self would offer.

The truth is, in that moment, in that space, you are free to choose how to respond. You are not tied to that emotional response that will probably make things worse. The more times you pause so you can respond optimally as the best version of yourself, the more you strengthen that optimal response pattern. It's an antifragility rep in the gym of life, taking a stressor and using it to make you stronger. Just like strengthening muscle, the habit of inserting a pause will strengthen over time. This tiny pause can change your life, as it did mine.

When you insert a pause, you can shut off, or at least tone down, the emotional part of your brain to access the logical, decision-making part. This opens up a chance for you to choose your optimal response, the response you'd expect from the best version of yourself: the most courageous, compassionate, and empathetic version—your wise, ninety-five-year-old self.

Let me tell you a story of one of my clients. We'll call him Tony. Tony is very successful. He recently sold a business for $50 million that he'd built from scratch. He has the dream home, literally. He also has a second and third home. He runs a few miles every day, and recently completed his first marathon. But what Tony didn't have was a great relationship with his youngest son, Matthew. We discovered it was linked primarily to how Tony responded to Matthew when Matthew wasn't at his best.

Matthew would do the typical things a six-year-old does. He wouldn't do exactly as Tony asked. He'd have tantrums and misbehave. Tony would get triggered and respond suboptimally, either by losing his cool, yelling, or acting in a way he'd later regret.

In our coaching sessions, Tony and I decided to go deep on "the pause" as it applied to his relationship with his son. Tony mapped out exactly what Matthew did that would trigger him. The behaviors, the situations, the attitudes. He visualized them. He visualized how he typically responded. And then we pressed pause on the mental video. Tony visualized how the best version of himself would respond in those situations. I asked Tony to clip out the suboptimal response from the mental video and edit in his best-self response, his optimal response. Then I asked him to replay the new mental video with his optimal response from the beginning (when Matthew would begin misbehaving) to the end (when Tony would respond in an optimal way) several times in his head. I encouraged him to really see it with his mind's eye.

Then Tony had the following task. He had to be hyper vigilant for those trigger situations with Matthew so he could practice his new response. I told Tony to look forward to those opportunities each and every day. To picture them as repetitions in the "antifragility gym" that is life. And just as each repetition strengthens a muscle in the gym, so would each moment of misbehavior in Matthew, provided that Tony completed the rep with his optimal response. And the secret to executing that optimal response, that new protocol, was simply to pause and create a tiny bit of space between stimulus and response so he had that moment of awareness to choose between an emotional, thoughtless response, and a more intelligent, thoughtful response. Creating a pause between stimulus and response was the pathway to that intelligence.

In a matter of just weeks, Tony's relationship with Matthew improved significantly, and he felt he was as good of a father as he was an entrepreneur.

Now, I'd like you to practice this for a moment. Think about the last time you reacted poorly to something. Picture how you might have responded had you inserted a pause. Whether as a deep breath, a silent count to three, walking out of the room, or simply taking a break from the situation. Would the best version of you have responded differently?

The next time the kids are bouncing off the walls as you try to get them to bed, or your daily routine is disrupted, or you receive that unexpected piece of news, or you're offered that sugar-filled dessert... pause. Create a tiny moment of awareness between the stimulus and response, so that you can access your infinite wisdom within. And respond as the strongest, wisest, most courageous version of yourself.

Because remember, in every situation no matter what it is, there will always be an optimal response, and then there will be everything else.

HARNESSING THE "STRESS" OF LOSS

Sometimes we encounter a Goliath on the battlefield in the form of a new goal, habit, or routine that we're trying (and failing) to attain or master. Such was the case for me when I was trying to embed the peak-performance routine I mentioned in chapter 5. To refresh your memory, I determined that the following five factors create winning days for me: getting eight hours of sleep, completing ninety minutes of high quality work by 7:30 a.m., exercising for at least twenty minutes by 8:30 a.m., shutting down my day by 6:30 p.m., and turning off all the electronics ("digital sunset") by 8:30 p.m.

The problem was that my success rate, the number of weekdays per week where I ticked off all five factors, was only 20%, or only one out of five days. No matter how hard I tried, there was nearly always a reason for not ticking all the boxes. The routine was about as fragile as it could get, and I needed something to make it antifragile.

Enter "Loss Aversion."

Humans hate losing things. It's wired into our DNA to help us survive. For example, the average person will find the pain of losing $100 significantly greater than the happiness associated with gaining $100. So how can we harness the stress we feel from loss? By simply putting some money on the line.

Behavioral scientists from Yale University have discovered that if you create a monetary penalty for not hitting a goal with a friend or an accountability partner, you will be up to five times more likely to achieve it.

Armed with this knowledge, I put some money on the line for not hitting my peak-performance routine. I had to pick an amount that would sting, an amount that I wouldn't dare let myself lose. I settled on $1,000. I also realized I couldn't go from zero to perfect, so I built in some buffer, settling on three out of five days, or 60% of the work week as the target for my peak-performance routine. If I ticked off all five factors in my routine, Monday through Friday, I recorded a win; if not, a loss. Any week that didn't result in at least three winning days would cost me $1,000, in the form of a donation to a peer group of entrepreneurs that also served as my accountability partner.

There was no way I was going to let myself lose that money, and my results immediately improved. What was a fragile routine, likely to break at any moment, suddenly became antifragile. No matter the adversity thrown my way, I managed to dig further in, hitting all five factors for at least three days, each and every week. I have not had to part ways with $1,000 since putting that money on the line. And in addition, I'm feeling better, stronger, happier, and more productive with my peak-performance routine in play.

So, do you have a dragon to slay? A particular goal, habit, or routine that's important for you, but that you can't seem to master or achieve? Choose a sum of money you wouldn't let yourself lose, place that "bet" with a friend or colleague, and watch yourself become a tank, blasting through any obstacles in your path.

ADAPTING BOLDLY TO CHANGE

In *The CEO Next Door*, three authors share the four learnable behaviors that transform everyday people into world-class leaders. One of them is a person's ability to adapt boldly to change. As authors Botelho, Powell, and Raz state, such leaders "have learned to welcome discomfort, conflict, and change." That certainly sounds like antifragile leadership to me.

This also begs a question: when the unexpected knocks on your door, how antifragile is your response? Do you adapt well to change? Do you adapt *boldly* to that change?

In 2018, the UK restaurant industry started to take a beating. Rapidly changing market conditions forced many of the nation's largest chains to close anywhere from a third to a quarter of their estates, with several brands disappearing completely. Chilango, the Mexican restaurant chain I co-founded, seemed to be bucking the trend as our sales growth continued to outperform the industry, culminating with a successful fundraise in 2019.

But just months later, we were forced to restructure our company as well. Several undeveloped sites, which we had decided to sell given the changing sector climate, began to burn significant amounts of cash when the purchasing parties (also spooked by the climate) decided to step away. Investments we had made in new sites, the head office, and various sales initiatives also failed to deliver their expected returns, while the rents in some of our existing locations materially increased. To make matters worse, our bank closed our overdraft facility, also citing sector concerns. It was a very painful experience, made all the more difficult by relentless media speculation about our future and a host of inaccurate stories and misinformation. Nevertheless, we managed to restructure our head office, many of our debts, and exit several leases, while preserving the principal investments of our investors and their rates of return within the new structure. Of course, with the benefit of hindsight, there are things we would have done differently, but the restructure restored the company's profitability, and we seemed to have adapted to the change.

Just three months later, though, the COVID-19 pandemic forced the closure of all our sites, and the company faced bankruptcy as we went from solvency to insolvency. Fortunately, the brand and restaurants were rescued by new owners to take it forward into the unknown, but the experience was incredibly demanding and difficult, to say the least.

Simultaneously, the coaching business I had recently started also took a massive hit, as many of the CEOs, entrepreneurs, and leaders I was serving were barely surviving the pandemic themselves. I had to pivot quickly, creating a free, 100% virtual event designed to help leaders not just navigate the crisis, but also emerge stronger—true antifragility. The only problem was that I had never run an event in my life, let alone hosted an online group of 200+ CEOs I had never met for nearly five hours. But this was precisely what I needed to do—step into the change and offer people a helping hand through it. Off the back of that event, several new paying clients emerged, restoring the coaching business's profitability.

Content marketing represented another bold adaptation. Many of my coaching clients had resulted from various speaking engagements at events in the UK and the US. When the physical event market collapsed I rapidly created content on my YouTube, Facebook, and Instagram channels to complement my LinkedIn presence.

These stories represent two of the primary ways the authors of *The CEO Next Door* suggest that we boldly adapt to change: learn to "let go of the past" while "building an antenna for the future." With Chilango, I had to let go of the past, and with the coaching business, I had to quickly build an antenna for the future.

So, how can you develop your ability to let go of the past? To start, you must be willing to discard the habits, strategies, and traits that have gotten you to where you are today. Ask yourself which practices or assumptions may be holding you back. Similarly, realize that a certain way of doing business in the past may not be the best way of doing business in the future. You must be willing to experiment with new approaches and ways of being, while also acquiring skills you don't have. By creating a new you, you are also letting go of the old you.

What about building an antenna for the future? One of the first things you can do is make sure you have reserved time for thinking about the future. An actual calendar appointment with yourself—including friends, family, and/or colleagues, as required. During such time, you can consider key trends, what changes are on the horizon, and how you are positioned against those changes or trends. In a business context, one of the powerful ways I build an antenna for the future is by speaking to my customers. Understanding their challenges, struggles, and frustrations, as well as what most excites them, informs the products and solutions we develop.

Darwin was right: "It is not the strongest of the species that survive, nor the most intelligent, but the one most responsive to change."

PRE-MORTEMS & POST-MORTEMS

As previously mentioned, some of my coaching clients include former US Special Forces operatives. Before engaging in any mission, and immediately following, these brave soldiers perform what you can call a pre-mortem and a post-mortem, respectively.

During a pre-mortem, the soldiers think through and visualize everything that could potentially go wrong during their mission, whether that's an enemy emerging from an unexpected location, a team member becoming injured, or some other undesirable event. Most critically, they also discuss and visualize how they will counter each and every obstacle that may appear. When it comes time for the actual mission, they can not only survive the shock of the unexpected, but actually step strongly into the discomfort, having already "seen" it and planned for it in advance.

Pre-mortems are a fantastic way to build antifragility into all aspects of your business and life. I often visualize all the things that could potentially go wrong in my day, including the typical things that might distract me and things that may not go the way that I had hoped. In my mind's eye, I see these events as they unfold, and then also visualize how I would respond, as my best antifragile self, in each and every situation.

At times, I've asked my team to conduct pre-mortems as well. I ask them to imagine a year has passed and we've failed. What would have driven the failure? We've then prioritized the obstacles, based on the potential severity and likelihood of occurrence, and developed plans to mitigate their risk.

Referring back to our Special Forces operatives, the post-mortem is equally powerful. Once a mission has been completed, the soldiers gather for a debriefing, also called an After-Action Report. Rank is set aside, and everyone is encouraged to speak their mind. The discussions can become heated as emotions fly, all in the spirit of helping one another learn from successes and failures so they can better navigate the future life-and-death decisions they will face.

Granted, most of us are lucky not to face such decisions very often, if ever. However, our days, projects, and "missions", if you will, are chock full of learning opportunities. Note those opportunities, embrace them, truly learn from them, and you will become antifragile in the process. Every single day, I perform a post-mortem on the day itself, reviewing the twenty-four hours just past and asking myself what went well, my wins, and what could have gone better, my learnings. What did I win? What did I learn? I also do this on a weekly and quarterly basis, as mentioned in "Measure & Monitor" in Part 2 of the book.

Billionaire hedge-fund manager and philanthropist Ray Dalio attributes much of his success to performing post-mortems on a regular basis. Ray quickly translates failure into learning and becomes stronger as a result—the hallmarks of antifragility yet again.

In his best-selling book *Principles*, Dalio takes us through a five-step process involving Goals, Problems, Diagnosis, Design, and Doing. I've found the process below to be helpful for both me and my coaching clients:

1. Set clear goals.
2. Identify the problems that stand in the way of achieving your goals.
3. Diagnose the problems to understand their root causes.
4. Design plans or solutions to overcome the problems.
5. Do what's necessary to push these designs through to results.

We begin with a goal, and then run into a problem. We then need to diagnose the problem and really understand the primary issues that are driving it. Then we're ready to design solutions to these issues, which we bring to life by taking action. As we move through the loop from setting exciting goals, to failing, to learning, to improving, to setting even bigger goals, we become antifragile. We turn challenges into growth opportunities.

Pause for just a moment and consider the following:

1. What's your most important goal right now?
2. What obstacles or problems stand in the way of achieving that goal?
3. Think about the factors that are creating this problem. What's really driving the issue?
4. How might you overcome this issue? Design a solution.
5. When can you take action to implement the solution?

Regardless of whether we employ a pre-mortem to anticipate our obstacles or a post-mortem to learn from our experiences, we must take action.

If we do not act on our insights, we miss our opportunity to become antifragile, turning stress into strength. And even if we do take action, we often can't navigate everything on our own.

HIRE A COACH

Imagine the following: Michael Jordan, Venus Williams, or David Beckham, midway through the season, turns to the sideline and says, "Hey Coach, I think I got things from here. You can take the rest of the season off."

It would never happen, right? If even the very best need a coach, to both get to and stay at the top, what does that say about the rest of us?

When you study people who have truly mastered their craft and are at the top of their game, one thing you will always find is that they didn't do it alone. Behind every top performer is a coach. Coaches provide the support and accountability needed to stay the course and navigate the unknown as we aim for the top.

Coaching has been a secret weapon of mine for years, helping me not only achieve my best, but also rebound from difficult times. A coach will bolster your antifragility by both supporting you and holding you accountable. They will cheer you on while also asking you the tough questions no one else dares to ask. A coach is an impartial counsel, providing the camaraderie and challenge you need.

When choosing a coach, make sure that you pick someone who has actually done what you are trying to do. You need someone who can advise you from the trenches, not the ivory tower. For example, I have always hired coaches who have built businesses themselves and held the CEO position, because that mirrors what I've done in my own life. Choose someone who you also connect with emotionally. If you're doing it right, you will be spilling your guts to this person and need to make sure they "get" you on a deep level. Choose the right coach and they will take your antifragility to the next level.

PART 2 ACTION STEPS

1. Think about your health, work, and relationships. Where do you find the biggest gap between your desired identity and your behavior?
2. If you were to define your best-self identity in each of the three domains, what words would you use?
3. List a champion proof for each best-self identity to know you've stepped into that identity every day.
4. What does your ideal day look like?
5. What does your ideal morning routine consist of?
6. How can you restructure your days to better manage your energy and time? Remember to be creative before reactive.
7. What is a massive goal you can set to force yourself to take massive action in your life? Don't be afraid to dream. Commit before you're ready.
8. What is one thing in your life you can 80/20? Zero in on the 20% of effort that would create 80% of the results.

9. Could you benefit from the power of single-tasking? Consider creating a timesheet to record how much time you spend on each task everyday and notice how much task-switching is costing you.

10. What is one stat in your life you can begin to monitor to help you stay on track and feel encouraged as you see your progress?

11. Implement a weekly review. Note your big wins, progress on your Top 3 objectives, what went well, and what didn't. Look ahead to your appointments for next week, review your Top 3 objectives, and mark time on your calendar to do them.

12. Which of the antifragility concepts most resonated with you? Is there a situation where you can apply that concept in your daily life?

THE THREE ALARMS

Part 3

8

INTRODUCTION TO THE THREE ALARMS

In Parts 1 and 2, we covered why peak performance is a worthy pursuit, the common pitfalls to avoid, and the habits that are key to success. Now we're going to put it all together in what I can almost guarantee is the simplest system for change you've ever come across. I've mentioned alarm-setting throughout the book, but in this part, I want to dig deeper into this method and show you how it provides a foundation for you to achieve your best in the three areas of life that matter most: your health, your wealth (which I also refer to as your work), and your relationships.

The three-alarm method is a way to segment your day across these three domains. Through the use of simple phone alarms, you can remind yourself of what your best looks like. When the alarm goes off, you can think of yourself as stepping into that new identity—transforming into you at your best within that area.

If you're not completely following what I mean, go ahead and grab your phone right now. Open up your clock app, and begin setting up a new alarm, just as you would do when setting an alarm for tomorrow morning. As you create a new alarm, you'll notice a field that says Alarm Name or Label. Give the alarm a name. When the alarm sounds, the name you've given it will appear on your phone.

I have the following best-self identities set up as alarms on my phone:

- 6:30 a.m. World Fitness Champion
- 9:00 a.m. World's Best Coach
- 6:30 p.m. World's Best Husband & Father

As discussed in Chapter 4, I have a set of values connected to each of my identities that helps guide how that version of me behaves. I also like to think that each of these identities represents a champion version of me, so every morning, I also choose my "champion proofs." These are the simple actions that I take to "prove" that I'm showing up at my best. So whereas my three identities and the associated values are static, my champion proofs are dynamic, changing as needed in the context of a particular day.

Take a moment right now to think of you at your best on the health front. Give yourself a name. It could be a phrase like mine above, or the name of another person. For example, if you're into swimming as your primary health identity, perhaps you become Michael Phelps when it's time to get into the pool.

Similarly for work, who are you at your best? Once again, you could choose a name or a phrase.

Lastly, when it comes to your home life or your relationships, what does your best look like? How can you best capture that version of you showing up in the world? Above all else, make sure all of your three identities are aspirational for you. You should feel a force that pulls you to a higher place.

Each of my identities represents me at my best across the health, work, and relationship domains. I become these people, if you will, to power the relevant segment of my day. Exercising in the morning provides an energy boost that I enjoy for most of the day. So at 6:30 a.m., it's all about health, and it's the "World Fitness Champion" version of me who goes to the gym in the morning.

Come 9:00 a.m., I've transitioned to work, and it's the "World's Best Coach" taking over the reins.

Lastly at 6:30 p.m., it's time to show up as my best for my wife and kids, which I equate to showing up as the "World's Best Husband & Father."

This isn't to say that I no longer care about my health after 9:00 a.m. Or that I wouldn't want to show up at my best for my wife and kids before 6:30 p.m. I simply think of various segments of my day having a primary best-self identity.

Am I really the world's best at all of these things? Of course not. But by being intentional about what best looks like, using my phone to remind me, and acting as if I already am these people, my life is far more fulfilling. And by constantly reminding myself what the best version of me looks like, in the three areas of life that matter most, I'm more likely to actually show up as my best.

When you first implement this method, you may be very reliant on the alarms. They will startle and surprise you, catching you off guard. Over time, the daily alarms will begin to embed the identities in your subconscious. Your alarms will begin going off in your mind when you realize you're not acting in congruence with one of your identities. Or you may feel a moment of decision, when you could choose to respond as your best-self identity, or as something less. Perhaps you'll recall your health identity when you're questioning your stamina in the middle of your exercise routine, or later in the day when you're offered that piece of chocolate cake. Moments before stepping into an afternoon meeting, your work identity may come to mind, which changes the way you walk through the door. And in that same meeting, your relationship identity may whisper some advice in your ear, when your spouse calls to ask if you could leave work early.

Of course, there will be countless times when you fail to live up to your identities. You'll miss your workout, not give it your all, or choose a donut instead of an apple. You'll fail to deliver what you promised to a colleague, show up late for a meeting, or produce mediocre work. You'll lose your cool at home, not chip in as much as you could, or listen poorly.

These moments will happen. They are normal.

The beauty of enlisting the support of your three best-self identities —your guardian angels, your dream team—is that you'll be much more aware of these mistakes, better positioning yourself to learn and improve as a result of them.

And here's the real exciting part. There will also be many times, ever-growing in number, when you look back at your day, or on a particular moment, and give yourself a pat on the back. You'll realize that you acted in accordance with the best version of yourself. You'll smile with radiant enthusiasm after doing your best.

These three simple alarms provide three massive benefits in the end:

1. They are intentionality drivers, prompting you to show-up as your best.
2. They offer wise counsel, helping you make the right choices in the moment.
3. They prompt reflection, as you measure your actual behavior against how you, at your best, are capable of behaving.

After some time, your alarms will naturally begin to sound in your head, and eventually, like training wheels on a bicycle, you may find that you no longer need them on your phone.

As a parent, spouse, and leader, in the absence of these alarms, I was at risk of coasting through life, falling victim to "the drift" that I mentioned in Part 1. Most people are fairly good with their health, fairly good with work, fairly good with their relationships. But fairly good doesn't lead to you realizing your full potential. It takes conscious effort to become all that you're capable of becoming.

In the pages that follow, I will take you through how my three alarms have positively transformed my life, and some of the challenges they've helped me endure. The dream team I've assembled, in the form of my three best-self identities, helps me rack up micro-wins on a daily basis, which create macro shifts over weeks and years. I'll also share some stories from others who have stepped up their game with their own three alarms.

By combining the three-alarm method with the key peak-performance habits covered in Part 2, you can live your healthiest, wealthiest, most loving life.

9

THE HEALTHIEST YOU

At 6:30 a.m., the first alarm on my phone goes off: *World Fitness Champion*. I'm not a World Fitness Champion, and never will be, but the phrase means something to me. That's who shows up at the gym in the morning. Especially the mornings I don't feel like going, I'm powered by the identity that I'm a pro, not an amateur. In fact, thanks to Steven Pressfield, one of the best ways I like to describe a professional versus an amateur is that a professional takes action whether they feel like it or not. Amateurs need to "feel like it" in order to take action.

A little bit before this first alarm sounds, I've already thought through each of my three identities. I keep this simple, thinking of each identity and the three values that I ascribe to each, and choosing a champion proof that will exemplify each identity in the context of that day.

When this first alarm sounds, I'm reminded to step into my World Fitness Champion self. The version of me that approaches my morning exercise with a relentless, pain-seeking, and varied approach. It's this version of me that will go after the champion proof I've chosen for the day, whether that's burning 500 calories on the stationary bike, completing ten sets of ten on the leg-press machine, or something else. In this sense, I'm intentional about who I am, how I will behave, and what I will do—or shall I say, what I "at my best" will do.

This identity not only powers my intentionality, but also provides the motivation to complete my workout or push myself a tiny bit more. For example, there may be that moment when I'm not sure I'll get past the eighth repetition on an exercise, and suddenly, this little voice goes off in my head that says, "And watch what Eric's about to do next—this is what separates champions from all the rest." Suddenly I can power through, hitting the ninth and tenth rep, before busting out the eleventh and twelfth for good measure. So my World Fitness Champion identity serves not only as an intentionality driver, *before the moment*, to push me to workout, but also as a motivational coach, *in the moment*, to help me cross the finish line. And when you're leaving the gym or returning home from your run, a sense of triumph comes over you, when you know that you showed up and delivered at your best.

Our health extends beyond an exercise routine, of course, but I've found exercise to give the biggest bang for the buck in the health department. It's the 20% of things I could focus on to deliver 80% of the results. When I exercise as a World Fitness Champion, I tend to act more congruently with that identity throughout the rest of the day. Eating the right foods, avoiding the sugary snacks, and prioritizing my sleep.

I do still have my moments—when temptation knocks on the door, masquerading as a bowl of ice cream or a late-night series binge, perhaps. But I've come to recognize these as simply weights in the gym of life. Antifragility moments when I can turn stress into strength. It's in those moments that I tap into the power of "the pause" from our friend Rollo May. I find that if I simply pause when presented with an unhealthy choice, I can create the space within which to summon my best self. "What would the World Fitness Champion do?" I often ask myself. The best choice becomes immediately obvious.

Of course, there are days when I don't feel like my World Fitness Champion self genuinely showed up at the gym—days when I've clearly made poor eating choices during the day or didn't get the proper sleep I know my body needs. But in true champion spirit, I simply pick myself back up and try again the next day. As you behave more and more consistently with you at your best, you quite literally reshape your identity, falling less and less, and rebounding more quickly when you do. And as you rack up your micro-wins day after day, your self-belief deepens, and marco shifts begin to occur.

One such macro shift for me was my blood pressure. Up to and following my near disaster on that plane, my blood pressure was hitting unhealthy highs. I won't bore you with all the details, but a healthy blood pressure is below 120/80 (where the top number represents the force of blood against your artery walls when the heart pumps, and the bottom the amount of pressure between the heart's beats). My blood pressure was sometimes as high as 166/105, which is not that far away from what they call a "hypertensive crisis"—or, in other words, "go see your doctor immediately."

The number-one risk factor for death in the world (according to the Global Burden of Disease Study) is high blood pressure. I had already counted myself lucky once, and I wasn't going to test the limits of my mortality again, so I decided to get my blood pressure under control once and for all. Armed with the will and determination of my World Fitness Champion identity, I began making small changes, which created a huge change over time.

One of the first nuggets my research yielded was the effect of alcohol on blood pressure. Although I didn't drink on a daily basis, I certainly enjoyed myself when I did! The problem with alcohol is that it creates an inflammatory response in the body, which also leads to unwanted weight gain, both of which are linked to high blood pressure. So, continuing my journey toward better health, I decided to stop drinking for a month-long detox. When I got to the end of the month, boosted by my new sense of accomplishment, I victoriously decided to try another. At the end of the second month, I challenged myself to a third, which eventually became five months. When I heard a friend say he was going to do a year-long no-alcohol challenge, my first thought was, "Gosh, how are you going to get through a full year? All the socializing and then New Year's Eve?" Even despite the fact that I had done a successful stretch of no alcohol, a year still seemed quite daunting. But I decided to do it despite my reservations. That year was certainly challenging, but it got easier as I went along. And when I got to the other side of it, I just kept going. That was three years ago.

Eliminating alcohol created a noticeable improvement in my blood pressure. Inspired by the positive changes, and once again fueled by my World Fitness Champion identity, I began researching other natural remedies. You can hear more about my blood-pressure regime by simply heading over to my blog at www.ericpartaker.com, but these days, I regularly consume flaxseed, hibiscus tea, and turmeric (with a touch of black pepper). I also try to avoid too many animal products and eat plenty of leafy greens. The end result is a healthy blood pressure below the 120/80 mark, all thanks to the micro-choices that led to macro shifts, powered by identity-driven change.

These days, I take the time to enjoy life. I eat healthy. I exercise regularly. My blood pressure is now in check. I don't drink, I don't smoke.

None of this would have been possible had I not been so resolute about making an identity-driven change and a commitment to myself. That first alarm at 6:30 a.m. every day not only prompts me to head out the door and work out, but is also a regular reminder to make a conscious effort to be my healthiest self.

10

THE WEALTHIEST YOU

A t 9:00 a.m., the next alarm goes off on my phone. When I was a CEO, it said *World's Best CEO*. These days, it says *World's Best Coach*. In both cases, I've chosen an identity that means something to me. Specifically, me at my best, on the work, or wealth-creation front.

Timed to go off at the start of my work day, this alarm prompts me to recall my professional values—decisive, inspiring, and reliable—and how I can best embody them as the World's Best Coach. How will that version of me show up for the CEOs, entrepreneurs, and leaders I coach, I ask? How will that version of me focus to finish a piece of writing or presentation that I'm working on? How will that version of me handle the potential setbacks and disruptions that may arise as I work through the day's commitments? Very differently than the ordinary version of me. After all, this is the extraordinary version of me.

The power of this intentionality is palpable. You can feel it and sense it within, as if you are truly summoning a force greater than you. Armed with this tenacity, I can more easily tackle my champion proof for the day. This may be, for example, delivering a transformational kick-off session for a new client, speaking at an event, or planning a new batch of videos for my YouTube channel—whatever would best prove that the World's Best Coach is firmly in the driver seat of that particular day.

During the course of my day, my identity continues to provide support, especially at those moments when I'm not feeling up to the challenge. I may lose my motivation to complete a task at hand, or notice my focus is drifting. The temptation to push something off until tomorrow may be looming.

And then I pause. I create a tiny bit of space between the temptation that's triggering a less-than-best version of me, and my response. And in that moment, I summon the World's Best Coach once again, ask him what he would do, listen, and then follow the instructions. Sometimes it is indeed to call it a day, but more often than not, it's to simply put my head down and keep charging ahead, champion-style.

Every time I act in congruence with the best version of me, I reinforce that identity. Whether that's doing things the right way to begin with, or pausing to summon "the reinforcements," if you will, winning little battles along the way. With every triumph, I become more and more the person I aspire to be.

Don't get me wrong: my work day hasn't suddenly become a perfect wealth-creating machine. I still have my moments when I question where some of my time went during the day, or when I knowingly procrastinate instead of intensely focus. But in the spirit of progress, not perfection, these moments have become fewer and fewer over time, and when they do occur, I rebound more strongly and quickly. Why? Because I'm not alone, and have the support of the World's Best Coach at my side, giving me all the intentionality and motivation I need. And the beautiful part is that *he* is *me*.

As you continue racking up daily wins, the bank balance of your work identity grows over time. Each day represents a deposit into your best-self account, and like compounding interest, those micro-deposits eventually add up to macro shifts.

As the CEO of the restaurant chain I co-founded, I noticed a few gaps in my leadership. It's one thing to start a company—it's another thing to successfully scale one. When voicing my concerns to my coach, he recommended that we shoot for a big goal. Not long after that conversation, I saw a CEO of the Year award and thought, *Well, that would be a bit overkill, but why don't we try to win that?* My coach enthusiastically agreed.

I went to work to identify what made a world-class CEO, creating my own CEO bootcamp in process. As previously mentioned, I interviewed top-performing CEOs to better understand what drove their success. I read over fifty books on leadership, peak performance, and what it takes to be a great CEO. I also began soliciting my team more regularly for feedback. After all, if you want to improve as a leader, ask those you're leading.

I didn't improve overnight. I worked against this goal on a daily basis, little by little over a two-year period. My deliberate focus was powered by my identity at the time, the World's Best CEO, which went off on my phone every day. Years before winning the award, I decided to act as if I had already won. As if I already was the World's Best CEO on a day-to-day basis. And my daily choices and behaviors culminated in receiving the CEO of the Year recognition.

So what does the best version of you look like on the work front? Give it a name. Create an alarm. Start behaving more and more like that person every day, and soon, you'll be on your way to creating the wealthiest you.

11

THE MOST LOVING YOU

A t 6:30 p.m., the most important alarm of all goes off: *World's Best Husband & Father* appears on my phone, prompting the question, "How would the world's best husband and father walk through that door right now?" Of all three of my alarms, this one was the complete game-changer for me, and it was very much needed.

A few years after the plane incident, I thought everything was going fairly well. But my wife telling me she was leaving if I didn't change my ways was the ultimate wake-up call. She told me that even when I was around, I didn't actually "see" her. That I wasn't really present, and that I certainly wasn't doing my best as a husband and father.

Looking back, I had clearly become lazy and had started taking my marriage for granted. I'd get home after a long day of work, and my wife might ask for help with something, or want to talk, but I'd want to push it to the weekend. The kids would want to play, but I often wouldn't "have the time," choosing to work instead. Is that how the world's greatest husband and father would respond to his wife and kids? Of course not. The truth was, when it came to my most important relationships, I was still miles away from showing up at my best.

The timing of this wake-up call couldn't have been better. My wife had had a hugely positive impact on me, and there was no way I was going to let her down. The idea of the three alarms, and most importantly that third alarm, now really took flight. I had somebody worth fighting for, and when it came to the home front, I knew exactly what my best-self identity should be.

Every day when I see "World's Best Husband & Father" appear on my phone, I'm reminded to be the loving, playful, full-of-laughter person my wife and kids adore. Timed at 6:30 p.m., it quite literally changes how I show up for my family. But the changes on the home front, and their effects, happened much more gradually than I experienced with my other alarms and identities. It wasn't like my health, for example, where my blood pressure was finally normal again and my heart symptoms had disappeared. And it wasn't like winning CEO of the Year, either—I certainly haven't come across a Spouse & Parent of the Year award!

As previously mentioned, I start my day by reconnecting with each of my three identities. My dream team. My guardian angels. And a key part of that ritual is choosing my champion proofs for the day. On the home front, my champion proofs typically consist of the little things like telling my wife I love her, writing her a nice email or handwritten note, or taking time to have a coffee together. For my boys, it might be playing a game together, reading a book, or sharing how proud I am of them. On a daily basis these micro-wins, these small moments of love and appreciation, begin to add up. Although there may not be a giant trophy at the end of the tunnel, these proactive choices create monumental change.

Similar to my other identities, my relationship identity not only powers my intentionality, but also provides wise counsel in the moment, helping me significantly improve my reactions at home. For example, I may get into a disagreement with my wife, and in the past I might have let my anger or frustration get the best of me. But that rarely happens these days. As the seeds of a disagreement begin to sow, the World's Best Husband & Father comes to mind. More often than not, I'm able to pause in the moment and consider my response. And as this identity has become ingrained in my psychology, I am far more likely to catch myself before I misstep.

I also respond very differently these days when the boys ask to play or do something together, especially when I'm in the middle of something else. Countless times, I've paused, considered the question, considered me at my best, and then made the right choice. And just as I've experienced with the other identities, these better choices compound over time, like interest. Before you know it, you are behaving at your best with less and less conscious effort.

But once again, the changes happen very gradually. In a recent session with an entrepreneur I coach, I explained how your ability to respond as your best-self happens in five stages:

- Stage 1: Simple awareness. The mere act of defining what your best looks like on the relationship or home front elevates you to a different plane. You now have something to shoot for, and coasting through life is no longer an option.

- Stage 2: You continue to make mistakes, responding to the things that trigger you with a suboptimal response, as would your lower self. But afterward, you remember your best-self identity, and most likely shake your head a little bit, too.
- Stage 3: You experience your first moment of inserting "the pause," but your emotions get the best of you and you still respond in a less-than-optimal way. At least this time, you've managed to create that tiny bit of space.
- Stage 4: You've mastered "the pause," and eight times out of ten, you're able not only to create that space, but also to use it to choose a response congruent with you at your best, whatever that identity may be for you.
- Stage 5: This, for me, is the nirvana moment. A loved one does or says something that would normally trigger the worst in you, and *while* it's actually happening, you smile inside, already knowing the response—the response that your most loving self would give, without even the need to pause.

Even if you reach those nirvana moments, you will still find yourself falling down and making mistakes. But they will indeed become fewer and less severe over time. And when they do happen, you'll still respond as best as you can with some of the most loving words you can ever express: "I'm sorry." Why? Because that's how your best self would make things right, isn't it?

So as I said earlier, I'm not able to evidence my success in this domain with a trophy, particular result, or achievement. But I don't need to. The best evidence I have is what my wife says herself: that I'm a better man today than the person she met. And the love and affection from my boys says the same.

Deep down, I know that I'm a more loving person today, and I can feel that love in return. And if you take the time to define what best looks like for you, and gradually begin acting in accordance with it, you'll experience the same.

PART 3 ACTION STEPS

For each of the three domains, answer these questions:

1. For what time will you set this alarm?
2. What will you name it to represent you at your best?
3. When this alarm goes off, what are you likely doing? What decisions will you make?

Health:

Wealth:

Relationships:

CONCLUSION: LIVING AT THE SUMMIT

Becoming world class is not reserved for the elite. It's not some special gift for those born with certain privileges or advantages. Nor is it for the genetically superior. The 2% Club is available to anyone who wants it and will work hard enough and in the right ways. It is possible for anyone to achieve excellence in the areas of life that matter most.

The trick is this: you never fully arrive. There isn't a day when you've finally come into your most fully formed self. It is this constant pursuit of mastery that grants you access to this "club" in the first place, the unique position that Maslow referred to as the pinnacle of human potential. The willingness to acknowledge that you can continuously improve, and that you have more to offer, is the definition of mastery.

Mathematically speaking, mastery is an asymptote, like that word problem in high school you may remember where a frog is at the start of a dock and jumps halfway across, then jumps half that distance, and half of the remaining distance, and so on. When does he get to the end of the dock? Never. That's an asymptote: a line that keeps getting closer and closer to an axis but never actually touches it. That's mastery.

George Leonard calls this pursuit "being on the path" of mastery, continually getting closer to the goal but never quite arriving. Because, in the words of Gertrude Stein, "There is no there, there. You're just moving towards something. And that's the whole point of it."

That's the point of the three alarms: to be on the journey toward becoming your best self, embracing the imperfect days, integrating each leg of the stool into your daily practice, and always aspiring to greater things.

As a coach, my hope is to help others on their quest by offering what I've learned along *my* path—which I am still on, by the way. The simplest, most effective way I have changed my life is by realizing that a good life is not just about the work you do, the relationships you have, or even how fit you are. Rather, a good life is about seeing your entire life as a work of art that you get to create, and pursuing whatever that may look like for you.

A good life is one where you never settle, in which you are always challenging yourself to greater heights, using simple but proven tools for changing the way you think about yourself and how you act, treating productivity as a planning and execution practice, and learning to turn your obstacles into advantages. We are never done, never finished.

Even when we reach a summit, there are new peaks. I learned this many years ago, that you can be flying high and come crashing down, especially when you are living outside of your integrity. But if you embrace a more multifaceted approach to life, you can keep growing, keep reaching for more and better. And the reminders in life we all experience can be little alarms jogging our memory about what's important. May you—and I—never fall asleep at the wheel of our lives again, always knowing that better is possible.

A GIFT FOR YOU

One of the most common questions I get is, "Eric, can you coach and mentor me?" The answer is yes. I help people break through their barriers and reach their full potential, not just on the work front, but also on the health and home fronts, employing many of the principles discussed in this book.

If you would like to receive a collection of practical insights to help further embed these principles, simply send an email to the3alarms@ericpartaker.com.

And I'll leave you with this: following the emergency landing of that plane, I continued to experience symptoms, and I had to see a cardiologist for several years. But I reached a point when the symptoms went away completely. My cardiologist even said, "If I were to refer you to another doctor and not share your history, they wouldn't be able to find any issues with your heart. So, whatever you've been doing, keep doing it."

I know 100% that this is a result of having correctly implemented the peak-performance insights I've gathered over the last twenty years.

––––––

You see...
Every mistake you've made...
Doesn't matter.
The time that you've wasted...
Doesn't matter.
Who you were yesterday...
Doesn't matter.
You can achieve your full potential.
You can achieve your full potential with your health.
You can achieve your full potential with your wealth.
You can achieve your full potential with your relationships.
You can achieve your full potential...
... and it would be my honor to help you.

––––––

3 ALARMS STORIES

W hile writing this book, I spoke on many stages about the concept of the three alarms, and about various peak-performance principles. I also regularly discuss these topics in my weekly newsletter, which you can join at www.ericpartaker.com.

Below are a handful stories from my newsletter subscribers who wrote in to share their own experiences with the three alarms. I've changed names to preserve everyone's anonymity.

————

PATRICK

Eric, the impact of my alarms has been massive!

I set my health alarm for 6:30 a.m. and labelled it "70 Year Old Me!" I thought if the 70-year-old Version of me was there every morning, to show the impact of my poor health decisions, I wouldn't even consider those decisions in the first place. And it's worked!

I started waking up and exercising four days a week, which I hadn't done once in the previous two years. I no longer stopped at the gas station to grab a coffee and cinnamon muffin on the way to work. And throughout the rest of the day, I stopped eating any processed foods and bread. In a matter of three months, I've lost 25 pounds. Best of all I feel great, more enthusiastic, and more driven to do everything.

I set my work alarm for 8:45am and named it "World's Best Leader." The alarm brings intentionality into my work day, making me think about how the "World's Best Leader" would arrive at the office. Slowly but surely the company behaviors are changing... and ultimately that came from me deciding to lead differently and create clear accountability.

My last alarm is the same as yours, "World's Best Husband and Father," and was set for 6:30 p.m.. I have to admit this alarm is still a work in progress. When it goes off, I'm either still at work—which prompts me to go home!—or I'm on my way home and it makes me think about the evening ahead.

I know that with four kids, it can be very difficult for my wife at times. Simply recognizing this ahead of time changes the way I respond to things when I get home. I'm more helpful and have started coaching the kids in the behaviors we'd like to see.

———

BETH

Dear Eric,

I would love to share my story with you. After a very insightful call with you, organised by my office during this challenging time in our lives, I decided to give the three alarms a try. I have suffered with anxiety for years now, and only recently have been able to better manage it when it comes to work, but still find it very challenging when life throws you a million obstacles during a 24-hour day.

Often, I would get very overwhelmed, to the point where I would just freeze. I would lose focus on how to be the best partner and the best employee, while still working on myself inside and out. In a nutshell, I was not able to segment my life whatsoever, and when one thing fell apart, so did the rest.

So, after two weeks of using your three alarms, I am able to segment everything so much better, and it forces me to change my mindset from "Oh no, I have so much to do in every aspect of my life" to "Okay, I have a lot to deal with—so what can I do to become a better employee for the next eight hours and efficiently deal with every-thing that needs to be done?" I've also segmented my day with regards to my health and home life, asking myself the same sorts of questions.

Although this is probably not a groundbreaking story, I wanted to thank you for sharing something that has the potential to change my life, and I wanted to make sure you knew the incredible impact it has had on my anxiety and stress levels, and how it has already made me a better me.

FRANK

Hi Eric

I was deeply inspired by your three-alarms talk, and it was the first thing I put into practice after hearing you speak.

I set my alarms as:

5:45am - #runningeveryday—to ensure that I get up and run every day. I also have a Post-it written and attached to the phone so I am not looking at the screen but at a new affirmation or goal every day. I am now making a 300-mile charity cycle event happen!

8:30 a.m. - #creativityfirst—to remind me to CREATE before REACT when I get to work.

6:30 p.m. - #familytimeeverytime—reminding me to switch off and focus on my beautiful wife and three children. We have even now started a weekly family meeting (high-performing family!).

Sincere thanks for the learnings.

―――――

HENRY

Hi Eric

I heard you speak at the Pendulum Summit and really liked the three-alarms idea. It was a very simple but effective way to change my mindset during important parts of my day. As they say, you don't get a second chance to create a first impression. For me the three alarms are reminders to create my "first impression" for each day.

Each of my alarms gently reminds me that I can do better, as we all can.

9am "Grateful Leader": This reminds me to be thankful and kind (I take a minute to speak to someone different on my team each day), and to also lead by example by completing my two most important tasks of the day.

3:30 p.m. "Walking Man": I don't exercise in the morning and prefer the afternoon instead. This reminds me to take a break from the office (even if just for fifteen minutes) and go out for a brisk walk. I feel so much better as a result.

6pm "Family Man": My last alarm reminds me to be a great dad before walking into the house. I make sure I help out, listen better, and make our evenings fun together.

I can already see how much these alarms are helping me, and everyone else notices too.

Thank you.

ACKNOWLEDGMENTS

There are so many people that have influenced the conception of this book. I hope my memory doesn't fail me! Here we go...

Neil Fiore. 2014 was a game-changing year for me. I'm so glad I reached out to you after reading *The Now Habit* and *Awaken Your Strongest Self*. All the hours we spent together on the phone had a huge impact on me, especially with regard to centering, identity-driven change, and the language of choice.

Brendon Burchard. I appreciate all the advice you've given me over the years. The big things, like creating consistent success at work, without sacrificing my health and relationships. And the little things, like attaching values to the different domains in life, and making sure I start my days creatively, producing quality work, and not in the inbox! I will always remember our lunch in Puerto Rico!

Pat Flynn. Thank you for inviting me on your SPI podcast to discuss the concept of the 3 Alarms and many of the ideas in this book. Having to discuss my ideas live, in the final stretch of writing, helped me further structure my thinking. Much appreciated!

Rich Litvin. You have been a force multiplier in my life. After our time together, I had the confidence to not only go big, but to also slow down (to go fast!). Thanks for the time you took out of your busy schedule to help me through a pivotal and challenging period, and for all the coaching tools you gave me.

Brian Johnson. Your brilliant work helped me structure, name, and scientifically validate so many practices I had collected over the years. Especially with regard to my identities, values, and "champion proof" practice. Your energy, work, and love model positively reinforced my focus on health, wealth, and relationships. I have so many great memories from our calls together. Thank you.

Michael Balchan. I'll always remember "take rapid, V1, imperfect action" from one of our calls, encouraging me to live up to my favorite saying by John Burroughs, "Leap, and the net will appear." Thanks for reminding me that I had already won the award before actually winning it.

Todd Herman. I'll always remember our breakfast together in London, and all the great advice you gave me. Thanks so much for pointing out what you thought was the big idea within this book, and for helping me realize I already had the book's name!

Verne Harnish and David Haimes. Thank you both for pushing me to write a book far before I ever felt I was ready. What would have taken five years to "get around to" took only one year in the end.

Dan Houghton. You have been an incredible friend and business partner over the years. I appreciate everything you have done for me and all the experiences we've shared together. I've learned so much working with you, and I look forward to whatever the future may hold.

Tom Spathis. So many of the experiences I've written about in this book would have never happened without your friendship and generous support. When my back was against the wall, you were there. And more than once. Thank you.

Chris Moore. Likewise, so many experiences in this book would never have been possible without your friendship and support, during the highs and the lows!

Luis Castro. You have always gone beyond the call of duty as a friend and colleague. Thank you for helping me rebalance my life. You were there for the low points and helped me get back to the high points.

Jeff Goins. Thank you for believing in me and the idea behind this book. And for helping me turn it into a reality!

Liz Morrow. I know you have helped so much behind the scenes, and I'm incredibly grateful for your support. Thank you!

Michael Stetina, Stephane Neves, and Nasos Papadopoulos. Thank you for making the book's launch a reality!

Mom and Dad. You both mean the world to me. Thank you for the determination and perseverance you blessed me with. I love you both!

Gisele, my beautiful wife. Without you, none of this would have been possible. I love you.

ABOUT THE AUTHOR

Eric Partaker is a peak-performance expert, coach, mentor, and motivational speaker. He was named CEO of the Year at the 2019 Business Excellence Awards, one of the "Top 30 Entrepreneurs in the UK 35 and under" by *Startups Magazine*, and among "Britain's Most Disruptive Entrepreneurs" by *The Telegraph*. His work has been featured on seven major TV stations, in the *Wall Street Journal* and *The Economist*. He has also appeared as a guest judge on The Apprentice with Lord Alan Sugar.

Over the last twenty years, Eric has advised Fortune 50 CEOs while at McKinsey & Company, helped build Skype's multi-billion dollar success story, and co-founded the Mexican restaurant chain Chilango.

Eric is also a certified High-Performance Coach from the High-Performance Institute, and he completed a coaching certification and apprenticeship with Professor BJ Fogg, who leads Stanford University's Behavior Design Lab. He also continues to research evidence-based studies in psychology, neuroscience, habit change, leadership, and peak performance, and he coaches a limited number of entrepreneurs and leaders throughout the world, helping them reach even higher levels of performance, in both their businesses and lives.

You can learn more and subscribe to his weekly peak-performance insights newsletter at www.ericpartaker.com.

Printed in Great Britain
by Amazon